VILLAGE
MOTHERS
CITY
DAUGHTERS

The **Institute of Southeast Asian Studies (ISEAS)** was established as an autonomous organization in 1968. It is a regional research centre dedicated to the study of socio-political, security and economic trends and developments in Southeast Asia and its wider geostrategic and economic environment.

The Institute's research programmes are the Regional Economic Studies (RES, including ASEAN and APEC), Regional Strategic and Political Studies (RSPS), and Regional Social and Cultural Studies (RSCS).

ISEAS Publishing, an established academic press, has issued almost 2,000 books and journals. It is the largest scholarly publisher of research about Southeast Asia from within the region. ISEAS Publishing works with many other academic and trade publishers and distributors to disseminate important research and analyses from and about Southeast Asia to the rest of the world.

VILLAGE
MOTHERS
CITY
DAUGHTERS

WOMEN AND
URBANIZATION IN
SARAWAK

EDITED BY

HEW Cheng Sim

ISEAS

INSTITUTE OF SOUTHEAST ASIAN STUDIES
Singapore

First published in Singapore in 2007 by
ISEAS Publishing
Institute of Southeast Asian Studies
30 Heng Mui Keng Terrace
Pasir Panjang
Singapore 119614

E-mail: publish@iseas.edu.sg
Website: http://bookshop.iseas.edu.sg

The responsibility for facts and opinions in this publication rests exclusively with the editors and contributors and their interpretations do not necessarily reflect the views or the policy of the publisher or its supporters.

ISEAS Library Cataloguing-in-Publication Data

Village mother, city daughters : women and urbanization in Sarawak / edited by HEW Cheng Sim.
  1. Women—Malaysia—Sarawak—Social conditions.
  2. Women—Employment—Malaysia—Sarawak.
  3. Urbanization—Social aspects—Malaysia—Sarawak.
  4. Rural-urban migration—Social aspects—Malaysia—Sarawak.
  I. Hew Cheng Sim.
  II. Ttle: Women and urbanization in Sarawak
HQ1750.6 Z8S2V71   2007

ISBN 978-981-230-415-5 (soft cover)
ISBN 978-981-230-416-2 (hard cover)
ISBN 978-981-230-572-5 (PDF)

Typeset by Superskill Graphics Pte Ltd
Printed in Singapore by Photoplates Pte Ltd

Contents

Preface

Research in Sarawak is often fuelled by anxieties that oral traditions, cultural mores, customs and practices of remote rural communities will soon be lost by ever-engulfing modernization forces. Thus, most research focuses on rural ethnic communities, documenting rich indigenous cultures and customs and discussing the state's colourful history. However, if I were asked to pick only one aspect of social transformation in Sarawak which I believe to be the most significant, it would be the rapid rate of urbanization. In other words, it is argued that the hotbed of change is in the ever-expanding towns and urban centres as they pull more and more women and men from the hinterland of Sarawak. Very little is known of the experiences of Sarawak people in the wake of such unprecedented economic and social transformation and even less is studied of women's lives as they walk the tight-rope of change. In order to fill the knowledge gap, the few women who have conducted studies in this area held earnest discussions as to how to put together a small volume. We felt that a book of this nature will make an important contribution to studies of Sarawak in the late twentieth and early twenty-first century as so little work in Sarawak focuses on women.

All the contributors to this book are scholars who have lived in Sarawak for many years and therefore have an intimate knowledge of local conditions. This book is multi-disciplinary, and different methodological perspectives are brought to bear on the same subject matter, that is, women's experiences of rural–urban migration and urbanization. It is also empirically driven with material grounded in ethnography, field observation, case studies, surveys and in-depth interviews. Any shortcomings of such pluralism are compensated by the richness of the data and the tight focus of the book which makes women visible in the process of social transformation. What are the gendered experiences of different groups of women — women in the urban labour market, women who are sole parents, elderly women, women with mental illness? In other words, this book puts women's experiences centre stage and in the spotlight and gives development in Sarawak a gendered face.

In putting this book together, I would like to thank the contributors for their patience, the Faculty of Social Sciences, Universiti Malaysia Sarawak for hosting our meeting, the anonymous ISEAS reviewer for his/her valuable comments and suggestions, Triena Ong and her team at ISEAS for their efficient handling of this publication, and last but not least, my husband, Tang Tieng Swee for the photographs on the cover.

Hew Cheng Sim

The Contributors

Adela BAER received her Ph.D. from University of California, Berkeley in 1962. She was Fulbright Professor in Universiti Malaya in 1967–68 and in Universiti Malaysia Sarawak (UNIMAS) in 2001. She has held various positions in universities in the United States, India and Malaysia between those years. Her recent publications include *Vital Signs: Health in Borneo's Sarawak* (Maine, 2006) and *Genes, People, and Borneo History* (Maine, 2005).

Poline BALA is a Ph.D. candidate currently pursuing a degree in the Department of Social Anthropology, University of Cambridge.

Sara Ashencaen CRABTREE, Ph.D., is presently working in the Department of Social Work at the Chinese University of Hong Kong, where she is conducting research on Muslim ethnic minorities in the region. She has published widely in the area of mental health, as well as in cross-cultural social work practice and education. She is now writing two books: one being a co-authored volume on Islamic perspectives in social work; while the other expands on the current topic in this volume, that is, gender, post-colonialism and mental health in Malaysia.

GOY Siew Ching is a lecturer at the Faculty of Social Sciences, Universiti Malaysia Sarawak (UNIMAS). Before joining UNIMAS in April 2005, she lectured at University Technology MARA, Sarawak Branch. Her research areas have included labour employment, mobility and earnings. Her recent articles include "Male-Female Earnings Differentials in Kuching Urban Labour Market", in *International Journal of the Humanities* 3, no. 8 (2006): 171–80 (co-authored with Low Kuek Long).

LING How Kee has a doctorate in social work and social policy. She is currently the Head of the Department of Sociology and Anthropology, Faculty of Social Sciences, Universiti Malaysia Sarawak (UNIMAS). She was a social worker in the State Social Welfare Department, Sarawak for thirteen years before joining academia in 1994. Her areas of interest include women, community development and indigenization of social work practice. Her recent articles include "The search from within: Research issues in developing culturally appropriate social work practice", in *International Social Work* 47, no. 3 (2004): 336–45; and "Drawing lessons from local designated helpers to develop culturally appropriate social work practice", in *Asia Pacific Journal of Social Work* 13, no. 2 (2003): 26–44.

LOW Kuek Long is a lecturer at the Faculty of Business and Administration, University Technology MARA, Sarawak Branch. He has done research on labour employment, mobility and earnings. His recent article include "Male-Female Earnings Differentials in Kuching Urban Labour Market", in *International Journal of the Humanities* 3, no. 8 (2006): 171–80 (co-authored with Goy Siew Ching); and "The Roles of Employees Provident Fund in the 21st Century", in *Jurnal Akademik* (December 1996).

The Editor

HEW Cheng Sim, Ph.D., is an Associate Professor at the Universiti Malaysia Sarawak (UNIMAS). She is currently the Deputy Dean of Postgraduate Studies and Research in the Faculty of Social Sciences. Her research interests include gender relations, urbanization, marriage, family and work with a focus on Sarawak. She has published widely and her most recent book is *Women, Workers, Migration and Family in Sarawak* (London: RoutledgeCurzon, 2003).

1

Urbanization in Sarawak
A Context

Hew Cheng Sim

Introduction

In 2000, the Southeast Asian population was 37 per cent urban but it has been estimated that by the year 2017, the urban population in Southeast Asia will be 50 per cent. In Malaysia, the rate of urbanization has been even more rapid, from 34 per cent of its population being urban in 1970, to 50 per cent in 1990 moving towards 58 per cent in 2000. This is expected to reach 64 per cent by the year 2010 (Jones 1997, p. 238). In the Malaysian state of Sarawak, only 16 per cent of the state's total population lived in urban centres in 1970 and this increased marginally to 18 per cent in 1980. Then it jumped to 22 per cent in 1991 and 48 per cent in 2000 (Ishak Shari et al. 1997, *Yearbook of Statistics Sarawak*, 2000 and 2003). The Iban and the Bidayuh make up the two largest group of rural migrants. The majority of rural migrants are single with 45 per cent being females. More than half are between fifteen and thirty-four years of age. The major receiving centres are Kuching, Miri, Bintulu and Sibu in descending order of number of migrants. Kuching as the capital and administrative centre of the state has a population of about half a million. It has a large service sector that attracts the highest number of rural female migrants in Sarawak. In the main, manufacturing in Kuching is small to medium size and light industry rather than heavy. In contrast, male migrants are attracted to the petrochemical industries in Miri and Bintulu and to the wood-based industries around Sibu.

Jones (1997) argues that there are several observable trends which have led to an under-estimation of the levels of urbanization in Asia. First, urbanization has led to a blurring of what is considered urban and rural. Increasing penetration of infrastructural and economic development beyond city boundaries has resulted in what McGee (1991) calls the emergence of *desakota*, which literally translates into "village-town" in Asia. Globalization and the integration of village economies with the urban has meant that there is a reconfiguration of large zones around major cities which are known as extended metropolitan regions (EMRs). EMRs as a form of suburbanization (Yeung Yue-Man 2000) or ubanization of the rural areas (Jones 1997) have resulted in changes in land use, a proliferation of non-agricultural activities and therefore a greater variety of non-agrarian employment. As Jones (ibid., p. 239) pointed out, "The standard understanding of urbanization implies a high level of non-agricultural employment. But the fact is that in East and Southeast Asia, many areas defined as rural have high proportions of workers in non-agricultural activities." This is aptly put by the Chinese Government's slogan for in-situ urbanization, "leave agriculture but not the village" (ibid., p. 241). Often EMRs lie outside of official metropolitan boundaries and hence their rapid growth of urban activities has not been taken into account.

A shift from the primary to the secondary and tertiary economic sectors is also occurring in Sarawak. Between 1980 and 2003, the percentage of people working in agriculture, forestry, livestock and fishing dropped dramatically. It fell from 60 per cent in 1980 to 23 per cent in 2002. However, the service sector has seen an increase from 18 per cent in 1980 to 25 per cent in 1999, while manufacturing and construction has leapt from 10 per cent in 1980 to 22 per cent in 2002 (*Yearbook of Statistics Sarawak*, 2000 and 2003). Although no statistics are available on the size of the rural population involved in non-agricultural occupations, several developments can be observed. First, on the outskirts of urban centres, light industries have mushroomed. Many of these factories are located in close proximity to outlying villages in order to tap the cheap rural labour force. Second, as a result of improved roads, many commute daily on their motorcycles to their work-places in the urban centres while continuing to live in the village. When the phenomenon first began, it had a gendered dimension. Many of those working in light industries sited near their villages were women. The pay was low and therefore unattractive to men. Married women were less mobile because of their domestic responsibilities and were forced to take up whatever employment was available in the vicinity of their villages. Men, on the other hand, enjoyed greater mobility and preferred to commute to nearby urban centres where there were more lucrative employment. In other words, men previously made up the majority of daily commuters who travelled to the city for work. However, this is changing. As women get more schooling, they are able to move up the employment ladder to take up office jobs in towns and they too have joined the ranks of daily commuters. Families who are financially better off, have a "half-way house" on the fringe of the city where they live on weekdays and commute back to their "weekender" in the village.

Another trend which is often neglected in our understanding of the levels of urbanization in Asia, as pointed out by Jones (1997), is the penetration not only of urban economic activities but also urban amenities into rural areas. He argues that rural transformation is so vast that truly isolated villages are things of the past for the greater part of Southeast Asia. To a certain extent, this is true even for Sarawak. Villages sited at the periphery of urban centres have seen the greatest changes. Young and old now sit before the television set in the evenings, rather than telling stories and talking to each other on their verandahs as in the past. Television programmes offer more excitement than tales of a bygone era. Similarly, with the introduction of piped water, there is no longer the communality enjoyed while bathing in the river. Bathing now takes place in the privacy of one's home. Women in many "semi-rural" villages also no longer go out in small groups to collect firewood as many now cook with gas. Among family members, hand phones have replaced face-to-face interaction. In addition, with improved infrastructure, many people now own motorcycles, eliminating the long wait at bus-stops where people tend to meet and chat (Hew 2003*b*, p. 43). To a lesser degree, even in remote villages, television sets are ubiquitous possessions operated by diesel generators. I recall an encounter with a traditional blanket (*pua kumbu*) weaver in an Iban longhouse some years ago. I asked the weaver how the idea of the designs came to her. I naively expected her to say that the designs came to her in a dream. Instead, her reply was, "I saw it on TV last night." It suffices to say that the Bario Highlands (see Chapter 7), which epitomizes an isolated mountain village, now has Internet access.

Before some of the causes and consequences of urbanization in Sarawak are discussed, a broad sketch of the historical development of nascent urban centres in Sarawak is in order.

Framing Sarawak's Past: Nascent Urban Centres

According to Lockard (1987), Sarawak can be divided into three main zones — flat coastal plains which are swampy mangroves, a hilly, forested intermediate region and the interior highlands which border Indonesian

Kalimantan. Rivers are the arteries of life in Sarawak and the chief means of communication and transportation even today. They link all the three zones, with river banks being the sites of pre-modern settlements (1820–41) in the state (ibid.).

The ethnic landscape in the early nineteenth century basically mirrors these three main geographical zones. Muslim migrants from various parts of the archipelago settled on the coastal fringes while the non-Muslim indigenous communities occupied the intermediate hills and the interior highlands. The Muslim settlers were a highly mobile group and established trading posts at the confluences of major rivers and established ports at river mouths. They controlled riverine trade and communication and wielded considerable influence from the coast into the interior. The non-Muslim indigenous communities on the other hand, were largely shifting cultivators of paddy. Apart from the Muslims and the other indigenous communities, the Chinese form the third most important group of settlers in the state. Trade links between Sarawak and China dated back to the seventh and eighth centuries; archaeological digs at the Sarawak River delta near Santubong have revealed an extensive iron-smelting industry and Chinese beads and ceramics (Andaya and Andaya 2001, p. 11). The Chinese population grew considerably in the eighteenth and nineteenth centuries when they arrived to open gold mines or worked in retail as well as the export trade and artisans activities (Lockard 1987).

According to Cleary and Eaton (1992, p. 55), "The ethnic map was constantly shifting in response to indigenous and colonial stimuli". Under the Brookes (1841–1941), there was a rigid separation of the different indigenous groups, both in social function as well as in settlement patterns. Here, the two largest groups in Sarawak — the Iban and the Chinese — will be discussed. The Iban are believed to have migrated from the Kapuas Basin of Kalimantan to Batang Lupar in Sarawak as early as the mid-sixteenth century (ibid.). In five generations they occupied all the major rivers in the Kuching, Kota Samarahan and Sri Aman divisions of Sarawak. The early seventeenth century saw their migration into the Rejang river basin and eventually into lower Baram River (Padoch 1982). The Iban put up a fierce resistance against the Brookes but once crushed, the Brookes used them as a military force against other ethnic groups in the state. Small groups of Iban who acted as the protective force for Brooke rulers subsequently moved to various administrative centres in Sarawak.

In contrast, the Chinese were actively sought after by the Brookes at the end of the nineteenth century for the economic development of the state. They were at first earmarked to work in tobacco plantations but many became traders in small bazaars along the river and gold miners in Bau. A colony of Foochow farmers eventually settled around Sibu growing export crops like gambier, rubber and pepper. It was said that by 1909, there were 45,000 Chinese in Sarawak (Chew 1990). Slowly, they penetrated upriver trade and replaced the Malays. Once edged out by the Chinese, the Malays were given an even larger political and administrative role in the Brooke government. Hence, each of the three major ethnic groups in Sarawak had its own area of specialization. As Pringle (1970) succinctly described it, "The functions performed by Malay, Chinese and Iban were thus political, economic and military respectively".

One particular feature of Brooke rule was the construction of forts at strategic locations along the major rivers of Sarawak. The Brookes constructed some fifty forts (ibid., p. 65). Once a fort had been built, it acted as a nucleus for enterprising Chinese traders to build shop-houses around it. Hence Chew (1990) argued that the Chinese pioneers played a pivotal role in creating nascent urban centres in Sarawak. Cleary and Eaton (1992, p. 115) further argue that "cities like Kuching were largely colonial creations designed to facilitate the centralizing administrative and trading functions of the new state". Under Brooke rule, Kuching grew from a Malay village (*kampung*) of 6,000 in the early 1850s to 35,000 by 1939 (ibid., p. 117). Hence, trading and administrative networks were the start of small towns and bazaars in Sarawak. According to Lee (1962*a* in Cleary and Eaton 1992, p. 54), the population of Sarawak was a mere 141,000 in 1871. By the time of the first census in 1939, the population of Sarawak had grown to almost half a million (ibid). Brooke rule therefore transformed the pre-modern settlements into culturally heterogeneous towns and bazaars.

With this view of the past, we are now ready to examine the various processes that caused the accelerated rural-urban drift in present day Sarawak.

The Rural Side of the Migration Equation

1. Land and Forest Policies

The period of the Brookes in Sarawak saw the promulgation of many important policies affecting the rural economy. These have been consolidated and extended by the British colonial government (1946–63) and enforced up till today. Since Charles Brooke was eager to attract Chinese farmers to Sarawak, by the early 1900s thousands of Chinese farmers had arrived to settle in the lower Rejang River area to plant rubber. Although there were serious communal conflicts over Chinese encroachment on native arable land, the government of the day was reluctant to halt Chinese migration as it would mean a cut in revenue. Hence, two major land laws were enacted — one in 1931 and another in 1933.

Under these laws, land in the state was divided into Native Area Land and Mixed Zone Land. The former was further sub-divided into Dayak Areas and Native Reserves. Dayak Areas roughly corresponded to the present class of Interior Area Land, which is largely primary forest deep in the interior that cannot be held under title. Customary rights may be created only by the felling of primary forest with government permission. In other words, Interior Area Land belongs to the state. Native Reserves, in contrast, are similar to the present category of Native Area Land which is land held under title. Only indigenous peoples can hold titles to this type of land. Mixed Zone Land is titled land and anyone (both indigenous and non-indigenous) can occupy and hold title to this type of land. For the non-indigenous people like the Chinese migrants, this is the only type of land which they may own (Pringle 1970, p. 316).

The land laws of 1931 and 1933 were later made more comprehensive in the Land Code of 1958 which included two more categories of Native Customary Land and Reserved Land. Native Customary Land includes all lands held under customary rights that were created in the past by the felling of virgin forest. Under the present land code, new customary rights can only be created if the government issues permits for the felling of forest. Reserved Land, however, is state land reserved for protected forest, national parks and wildlife sanctuaries (Hong 1987, p. 53). With the enactment of these land laws, the migration of the indigenous communities into virgin forest for the purpose of shifting cultivation was severely curtailed. State restriction on the availability of arable land meant that land is frequently re-used without a sufficient fallow period as required by shifting cultivation. This leads to low yields and the inability of households with small land-holdings to sustain themselves.

Complementing these land laws were forest policies for the state's exploitation of timber resources. Forest in Sarawak is basically divided into two categories, that is, Permanent Forests and Stateland Forests. The former is further sub-divided into Forest Reserves, Protected Forests and

Communal Forests. As their names suggest, Forest Reserves and Protected Forests are protected for their timber and forest produce, and indigenous peoples cannot exercise customary rights over them. However, collection of forest produce is allowed when permission has been granted by the Forestry Department. Communal Forests, in contrast, are specially set aside for the use of settled communities, but this type of forest is smallest in terms of acreage. The second type of forest, Stateland Forest, is available for agricultural purposes but can be converted in status to Permanent Forest when the need arises. Logging activities are controlled in Permanent Forest areas by the Forestry Department (ibid.).

Timber export is an important source of revenue for the state and constituted 18 per cent of exports in 2003. The exploitation of the state's forests by the logging industry, coupled with the new system of land tenure, have led to expanding encroachment on native land and an increasing restriction on indigenous agricultural activities. The forest is not only used for swidden agriculture but is an essential source of food, medicine, fuel and construction materials. Thus, increasing pressure on the land and deforestation through over-logging means a shrinking natural resource base and greater poverty for the people as they become increasing unable to support themselves from the environment. According to Puthucheary (1988), the highest incidence of poverty in Sarawak occurs in the rural areas and among paddy farmers. This problem was aptly pointed out by Morrison, a colonial officer who was in Sarawak for two decades (1947–67):

> In my personal estimation, the main failures of the colonial period lay in rural development and land administration. Above all, there was a failure to overcome the intractable problems of raising living standards in the countryside to an extent that would encourage country people (especially the younger, educated ones) to remain in the countryside and maintain their heritage of independence and social and cultural cohesion. (Morrison 1988, p. 45)

2. Development of Large-scale Plantations

Cash cropping dates back to early 1889 when the Saribas Iban was introduced to coffee planting (Pringle 1970, p. 202). Charles Brooke had always been convinced of the inferiority of swidden agriculture as practised by the indigenous communities and tried to stimulate interest in smallholder cultivation of cash crops. The Brookes discouraged large-scale commercial plantations, which were characteristic of other parts of colonized Asia, as they were afraid that the alienation of large tracts of land to European planters would erode their own power base. Thus, in Sarawak, the production of export-based cash crops was in the hands of agricultural smallholders. In other words, cash cropping became an integral part of indigenous farming. The cultivation of cash crops not only catapulted rural farmers into a monetized economy, the penetration of the global commodity market into the rural village economy meant that cash crops like rubber, cocoa and pepper were vulnerable to global price fluctuations which can lead to a crisis in rural household incomes. It was therefore important for households to obtain an alternative source of cash income. Remittances from cash-earning household members represented one such source. As Gerrits pointed out, households with an alternative income source, such as remittances, were better able to stabilize agricultural production by investing their capital and labour resources in a variety of agricultural products. In this way they were cushioned from any crisis that was triggered by a fall in the prices of cash crops (Gerrits 1994, p. 284).

Cash cropping as a vehicle for rural development accelerated when Sarawak became a crown colony and this policy has been intensified since Sarawak's entry into Malaysia. The state's disdain for this method for swidden agriculture has led to a conviction that the panacea of rural ills lies in a development policy which emphasizes large-scale plantation cultivation of cash crops such as oil palm. It was hoped that the cultivation of cash crops in large plantations would increase the volume of agricultural commodities for export and hence increase the State's foreign exchange earnings. Also, lands owned by indigenous farmers that were developed into cash-cropping estates could provide dividends as well as employment for rural people.

However, unlike Peninsular Malaysia where there has been a large injection of funds into rural land development schemes especially for the poor and landless, the reverse has occurred in Sarawak. In Sarawak, the extensive smallholding agricultural system has instead been slowly eroded through a deliberate policy of encouraging private capital investment by large plantation corporations.

The drift to the urban areas has accelerated as many villagers are unwilling to work in the poorly-paid plantations when there are far more attractive employment options in logging camps and urban centres. The labour vacuum in the plantations has been filled by cheap Indonesian labour from across the permeable border. Hence transmigration of labour is a direct outcome of state rural development policies. It is ironic that instead of anchoring rural dwellers, state rural development policies have had the opposite outcome of becoming a catalyst for the rapid rural-urban drift (Hew 2003a).

3. Structure of Formalized Education

Another important reason for rapid urbanization is the structure of the educational system. The early Chinese migrants and Christian missions during the Brooke regime brought with them the early beginnings of schools. With colonial rule and Sarawak's entry into Malaysia, the process was accelerated. Increasingly, education is seen as an avenue for upward social mobility and a secure government job is much coveted. Education is a route to independence from farming, and it is the aspiration of many parents that their children be spared the hardship of living off the land. As mentioned earlier, remittance of wage-earning children also meant a less precarious livelihood should the paddy harvest fail and the prices of cash crops fall. Apart from parental aspirations, the organization of schools also promotes rural-urban migration. Primary schools can be found at village level but the majority of secondary schools are clustered in towns and bazaars. As infrastructure in Sarawak is poor, many secondary schools in semi-rural areas are boarding schools where food and lodging are provided free by the government. Thus, children from villages often spend their adolescent years away from their families, returning home only on weekends, once a fortnight or once a month and sometimes only at the end of the school semester. When schoolchildren return to the village, they are not initiated into the intricacies of farming (Hew 2003a).

In his study of the Iban, Sutlive (1984) suggested that a consequence of a formalized educational system was to encourage Iban migration to towns. He argued that traditionally, Iban children were taught informally *via* the use of tools and through folklore told by village elders on the longhouse verandah (*ruai*) after the evening meal (what Sutlive called the Iban "evening school"). With state schools now away from the longhouses and in urban centres, many Ibans are now no longer learning the values of their ancestors through oral tradition. Instead, they have internalized urban ways. Hence, the organization and location of schools have contributed to the rural youth being disengaged from their own communities. In addition, many of the young who have had more years of schooling than their parents feel that they know much more than their elders. Far from preparing them for life in the village, formal education has the reverse effect of alienating them from it. This is what one young female rural-urban migrant had to say:

> I don't even know how to hold a machete. (*Nak pegang parang pun tak tahu.*) My mother doesn't encourage us to farm. She doesn't want us to inherit her work. It is all right to farm for fun but not as a full-time job. She wants us to get a more secure job. In fact, she wants me to study and get a job with regular office hours. When we were all in school, my mother would not allow us to follow her to the farm when we returned home on weekends. My parents would only spend half a day farming on the weekends that we were at home. When I was in the village for a year before coming to Kuching, I tried to farm but could not stand the sun. (Hew 2003*a*, p. 106)

The depletion of natural forest produce through excessive logging, the increasing links between the rural agricultural base and the global commodity market, and the education of the young have all contributed to the accelerated rate of urbanization in Sarawak. Sutlive (1984) found that Iban men sought waged employment in logging camps and towns. Women left behind in longhouses faced even greater hardship as they struggled to support themselves and their children on exhausted land and depleted forests. Many women too migrated to towns in search of work. He estimated that between four to eight hundred Iban women worked as prostitutes in Sibu at the time of his research.

> They come from economically depressed rural areas. They range in age from twelve to thirty-five. They earn from RM150 to RM1,000 a month … They represent forty per cent of the Iban female population in Sibu. (Sutlive 1984, p. 13)

Thus, rural-urban migration is a gendered process with serious consequences for women.

The Urban Side of the Migration Equation

The availability of employment opportunities in urban centres has constituted a major reason for the unprecedented exodus from the rural areas. In Peninsular Malaysia, Yeoh (2001) argued that it was the New Economic Policy (NEP) of the 1970s with its preferential quotas in education, commerce and civil service employment which was the catalyst for Malay migration from the villages to the cities. In addition, rapid industrialization also drew the rural Malay populace to the urban labour market.

In Sarawak, rural men, especially the Iban, have a long tradition of migration for employment and social prestige. Freeman reported that "... throughout the year, about 20 per cent of the adult male population of an Iban community is absent on some kind of journey or enterprise" (1970, p. 225). As mentioned earlier, rural men frequently migrated to work in logging camps, sawmills and the petrochemical industry. However, it was the economic boom of the late 1980s and early 1990s which saw an accelerated rate of migration of rural women to the urban centres. The expansion of an urban middle class, increased levels of personal consumption and a change in lifestyle meant that families ate out more frequently and there is a greater demand for childcare centres as more and more mothers entered the workforce. This has resulted in greater employment opportunities in personal-services work in the urban centres for rural women migrants. In addition, since the late 1980s, there has been a government thrust to develop the tourist industry in the state (Hamid Bugo and Hatta Solhee 1988, p. 23). Revenue from tourist and travel agencies in the state jumped five times between 1989 and 2000. The percentage of women employed in wholesale and retail trade, hotels and restaurants also tripled, from 7 per cent of employed persons in 1980 to 21 per cent in 1999[1] (*Yearbook of Statistics Sarawak*, 2000 and 2003). The internal migration survey in Sarawak also found that 46 per cent of female rural-urban migrants worked in the wholesale, retail and hotel sector, another 36 per cent in community, social and personal services and only 15 per cent in the manufacturing sector. Although the majority of the migrants have an education up to secondary school level, the two main employment sectors that migrants enter, namely services and production or related work, were sectors which require little formal education (Ishak Shari et al. 1997, p. E.18).

Having dealt with some of the causes of urbanization, let us now look at some of its consequences.

Consequences of Urbanization

1. Gender Inequalities

In this section, three important aspects which concerns rural women migrants to the city are dealt with. First, rural women who worked alongside

their men as autonomous farmers in their own fields now find themselves
at the bottom of the urban waged labour market. The heavily segmented
labour market in Malaysia has led to great disparity in earnings between
women and men. In my own study (Hew 2001), migrant women who had
the same years of schooling (if not more), as their husbands, earned a mere
39 per cent of their husbands' monthly wages. Most of the women were
over-qualified for the type of menial personal services jobs that they did,
for example, waiting at tables, dish-washing, assisting in shops. However,
the majority of their husbands had additional credentials such as a driving
licence for trucks and other technical and mechanical skills. Gender wage
disparity and labour migration will be further elaborated in Chapter 2.
Labour segmentation is only one reason for the wage disparity between
wives and husbands. Another reason for their much diminished earning
capacity is women's history of interrupted employment as a result of
child-bearing and other domestic responsibilities.

This leads to the second point — the transformation of women from
autonomous rural farmers to dependent urban housewives (Hew 2003a).
In the village, childcare did not disrupt women's productive work in the
fields. They carried the young to the fields while others drew upon the
support network of kin and neighbours to assist in childcare. The role of
elderly grandmothers in childcare is discussed in Chapter 5. Women also
worked flexible hours and had control over the time and pace of work and
could incorporate childcare into their routine. In other words, in the
village, there was no clear dichotomous separation between domestic
work at home and productive work outside. In the city, migrant women
who marry and set up home do not have the support of kin and few can
afford childcare services. Thus, they become housewives who are totally
dependent on their husbands for survival. In the event of divorce or
abandonment, they are forced to return to their natal households in the
village or, alternatively, be separated from their children as they leave
them in the village to be cared for by kin, while they re-enter the urban
labour market. A new dependency on men has therefore emerged as a
result of urbanization.

The third point is that in the city, the opportunities and vulnerabilities
faced by single women migrants are different from those of their married
sisters. Single women migrants newly arrived from the villages experience
greater sexual vulnerabilities. In the study of single mothers as discussed
in Chapter 6 of this book, 14 per cent of 231 respondents interviewed
reported that they were abandoned by their boyfriends when they became

pregnant. In the village, the sanction for pregnancy is marriage and a suitor's promise of marriage is not easily broken as courtship is closely monitored and supervised by parents and village elders. Customary laws and village social mores are not enforceable in the city and many women are caught unawares when they first arrive there. Single motherhood is therefore a distinct possibility for young women migrants who do not understand the vulnerabilities that they face in an urban environment.

2. Urban Poverty and Income Inequality

The achievements of poverty alleviation in Malaysia[2] has been remarkable with the poverty incidence dropping from a high of 52 per cent in 1970 to 7 per cent in 1997 (Ragayah Haji Mat Zin 2004). However, there is a regional spin to this. Both Sabah and Sarawak recorded a higher incidence of poverty compared to the country as a whole. By 1999, Sabah had the highest incidence of poverty (25 per cent) in the country while Sarawak was the seventh poorest state in Malaysia with a 7 per cent incidence (ibid). However, Sarawak was slightly under the country's overall poverty incidence of 8 per cent.

The earliest data available for Sarawak showed a poverty incidence of 57 per cent in 1976. In the same year, urban poverty was 23 per cent and rural poverty was 65 per cent. By 1993, the state's poverty incidence has shrunk to 19 per cent, urban poverty incidence to 6 per cent and rural poverty incidence to 24 per cent. The fact that rural poverty has always been higher than overall poverty and urban poverty is a significant reason for the exodus from the rural areas (ibid.).

It is interesting to note that the incidence of urban poverty in Sarawak rose from 5 per cent in 1989 to 6 per cent in 1993. One possible reason for the increase in urban poverty in these years is the upsurge of migration of the rural poor to urban centres, adding to the number of urban poor. This certainly tallies with the discussion in the previous section on the expansion of the economy in the late 1980s and early 1990s which accelerated the influx of rural migrants into urban centres.

Although urban poverty has been much lower than rural poverty, income distribution in urban areas is more unequal. The same has been found in many other cities in Asia (Jones 1997). In the context of Malaysia, with increasing globalization and a move to more capital intensive industries as opposed to labour intensive industries means the wage gap between skilled and unskilled labour is widening. The availability of a large pool of lowly-paid foreign workers has further eroded any possibility of a wage rise amongst unskilled workers. As a result of this changing pattern of labour demand, wage differentials in the urban areas are widening.

Impressive as they are, the declining figures for the incidence of poverty means that what remains are the hardcore poor. The most vulnerable in this category are the Orang Asli in the peninsula, the interior indigenous groups of Sabah and Sarawak, the disabled, the elderly (see Chapter 5), and single mothers. The conditions of disadvantage — income insecurity, lack of access to proper housing, healthcare and education — are all mutually reinforcing. Take for instance, the case of a lowly educated, urban single mother as mentioned in Chapter 6 of this book, who could not earn enough to feed her family and is reduced to living in an urban slum where her home is surrounded by her neighbours' toilets. Poor sanitation led to frequent illness which further reduced her capacity to provide for the needs of her children.

Improving access to medical services and expanding healthcare facilities is critical especially in the context of rapid social transformation. Health issues such as sexually transmitted diseases brought home by migrant husbands and partners are all subjects of discussion in Chapter 3. In the end, an obvious point underlying the discussions in many chapters is the desperate need for a more adequate welfare safety net to cushion the vagaries of the market for the most fragile pockets in our society, the hardcore poor.

3. Political Change

In Malaysia, as in elsewhere in Southeast Asia (Jones 1997), urban centres such as Kuala Lumpur and Penang are hotbeds for oppositional politics. In the Klang Valley, which is a major destination for migrants, squatter colonies have been a major site of contestation. In the 1960s and early 1970s, urban slums were seen as "eyesores", "nests for criminals" and the official stance was that of eviction. However, this hardline position shifted when it was increasingly recognized that such deprivation could lead to political discontent. Yeoh (2001, p. 112) pointed out that "... in more established Malay settlements with a significant political vote-bank it would not be unusual to witness the whole range of basic amenities as well as kindergartens, meeting halls, and postal and telephone services." He went on to add that "the political fortunes of aspiring politicians are also tied up to these localities" (ibid., p. 113).

The observation that anti-government sentiments are often amplified in the cities can also be seen in Sarawak. In the recently concluded state elections in May 2006, opposition parties (Democratic Action Party and Parti Keadilan Rakyat) swept all four seats in and around the capital city of Kuching. The stunning victory by the opposition parties took the Sarawak United People's Party (SUPP) by surprise. The state government's silence over the renewal of land leases, corruption and a lack of transparency in government funded projects (prison and the State Assembly hall, to name but two) and ineffectual local councils all contributed to the defeat of the SUPP (*Borneo Post*, 25 May 2006). The political debacle led to recriminations with a Minister accusing City Hall for the high-handed way in which they handled illegal roadside hawkers (ibid.). The public rebuttal by City Hall as reported in the local press led others to join the fray (ibid., 28 May 2006). In the past, there have been incidents of skirmishes between City Hall enforcement officials and hawkers at one of the local markets. Poor rural migrants to the city often eke out a living through participation in the informal sector but are viewed as a nuisance by City Hall who sees only dirty pavements, traffic obstruction and disruption to social order. Thus, combating urban poverty, good governance and community development for greater equity are required to ameliorate the more dehumanizing aspects of urbanization.

Pattern of Women's Rural-urban Migration

According to Chow (2002, p. 20), women constituted about half of the one billion lifetime internal migrants in the developing world. In China, women outstripped men in the numbers migrating to the south of the country. In other words, there is an increasing feminization of migration, both internal and transnational. It is therefore not surprising that a lot has been written on women internal migrants in Asia, although much has been on factory women. Kung (1983) looked at migrant women workers in Taiwan, Trager (1988) in the Philippines, Wolf (1992) in Indonesia, Kibria (1995) in Bangladesh, Lee (1998) in South China, and closer to home, Ong (1987) and Stivens (1996) in Peninsula Malaysia. Stivens (1996, p. 160) in fact argues that there has been a long history of Malay women accompanying their migrant husbands to the cities. In other words, the migration of rural women to the cities did not begin with the new international division of labour or urban employment opportunities afforded by the country's New Economic Policy. However, what is distinctive about women's migration in more recent times is that family migration is increasingly replaced by individual migration.

Three theoretical perspectives dominate the literature on rural-urban migration. The first approach takes a structural-historical analysis of the causes of migration. This chapter has attempted to present this earlier. Elsewhere I have discussed the second approach which analyses individual decision-making (Hew 2003*b*). The third approach seeks to combine the first two positions and uses the concepts of households and social networks as an intermediate level of analysis. Households and social networks therefore link the individual to larger societal forces at work. In my own studies, women's rural-urban migration is not just a simple case of individual decision-making or of that of the household, but appears to be a mixture of both. This is particularly so for the women who migrated to help their families and for those who were ambivalent about migration but felt that they had little choice in the matter. At the same time, economic reasons were not the only narrative that I heard. Many women also spoke of their desire to experience city living and to become "modern". One young woman said, "To work in the city is more modern (...*kerja dipasar adalah lebih moden*) (ibid., p. 52). In other words, women also migrate for their own transformative projects.

Almost all the women that I interviewed found their first city job through introductions by kin and friends who were already urban workers. Thus, unlike those in many other countries, the women migrants in Sarawak did not join a pool of urban unemployed. Migration is therefore a complex process that involves not only the individual migrant but is enmeshed in social networks of kin and friends stretching from their rural villages to the cities. These social networks not only help new migrants find jobs but in some cases provide them with a place to stay when they first arrive in the city.

Rural-urban migration cannot be assumed to be a permanent process, and the uprooting that the word "migration" implies is not as drastic as it seems. Women migrants often return to help their parents in the village during crucial farming periods of planting and harvesting. Still others maintain links with their land in the village by sending remittances home to build houses or to start pepper gardens. In the face of a precarious urban existence, the land in the village and its social networks are insurance policies not to be taken lightly. In Jakarta, Murray reported that village houses were still maintained by migrants after forty years in the city

(1991, p. 67). Even when urban migrants rarely return to their village, they keep in touch through the comings and goings of other people. Village mothers also often travel to the urban centres to help out city daughters in childcare during critical periods in the life phase such as in childbirth and illness. Hence, there is a constant interchange between rural and urban which reflects the complex web of social networks in both locales.

Conclusion

This chapter has contextualized urbanization in Sarawak, outlining both causes and consequences. It has attempted to connect the past with the present, rural with the urban, government policies with individual actions. Non-Muslim indigenous rural women enjoy a lot of parity with their men under their customary law (*adat*), as they work hard in the fields to ensure that there is food on the table. However, in an urban labour market segmented by gender, the authority and standing that they previously enjoy is eroded. In addition, new dependencies are created when young mothers have no support networks in the cities. Urbanization therefore changed their gender contract with men and new inequalities are created. The opportunities created by urbanization largely benefited educated, middle class, urban women but disadvantaged their poor rural migrant sisters. The discussion in this chapter forms the backdrop for our understanding of women's experiences of urbanization which are the focus of this book. The rest of this volume looks at work, health, family and community which are crucial aspects of women's everyday lives as they negotiate the changing terrain of their world.

Notes

1. Employment categories by industry as used by the Department of Statistics, Malaysia remained the same from 1972–99 but changed in 2000. It is therefore difficult to make a comparison of figures before and after the year 2000 especially for this category of employment.
2. The Poverty Line Index (PLI) in Malaysia has long been contested. The PLI of RM510 per month for a household of 4.6 persons in the Peninsula, RM685 for 4.9 persons in Sabah and a PLI of RM584 for 4.8 persons in Sarawak in 1999 is said to be too low and unrealistic (Ragayah Haji Mat Zin 2004, p. 201).

References

Andaya, Barbara and Leonard Andaya. *A History of Malaysia*. Hampshire: Pelgrave, 2001.

Borneo Post. "Land Lease Issue Tops Reasons Given for SUPP's Loss, Land Lease Likely Cause of Defeat, Improve your PR, DBKU Told", 25 May 2006.

————. "Fadillah Takes City Hall to Task", 28 May 2006.

Chew, Daniel. *Chinese Pioneers on the Sarawak Frontier*. Singapore: Oxford University Press, 1990.

Chow, Ester Ngan-ling, ed. *Transforming Gender and Development in East Asia*. New York and London: Routledge, 2002.

Cleary, Mark and Peter Eaton. *Borneo: Change and Development*. Kuala Lumpur: Oxford University Press, 1995.

Freeman, J. D. *Iban Agriculture: A Report on the Shifting Cultivation of Hill Rice by the Iban of Sarawak*. London: HMSO, 1955.

Gerrits, Robert. *Sustainable Development of a Village Land Use System in Upland Sarawak, East Malaysia*. Unpublished Ph.D. thesis, University of Queensland, Australia, 1994.

Hamid Bugo and Hatta Solhee. "Macroeconomic Perspective of Sarawak — An Overview". In Abdul Majid Mat Salleh, Hatta Solhee and Mohd. Yusof Kasim (eds.), *Socio-economic Development in Sarawak: Policies and Strategies for the 1990s*. Kuching, Sarawak: Angkatan Zaman Mansang (AZAM), 1988.

Hew, Cheng Sim. "Of Marriage, Money and Men: Bidayuh Working Mothers and their Households in Kuching". *Asian Journal of Social Science* 29, no. 2 (2001): 285–304.

————. "The Impact of Urbanization on Family Structure: The Experience of Sarawak, Malaysia". *Journal of Social Issues in Southeast Asia (SOJOURN)* 18, no. 1 (April 2003*a*): 89–109.

————. *Women Workers, Migration and Family in Sarawak*. London and New York: RoutledgeCurzon, 2003*b*.

Hong, Evelyne. *Natives of Sarawak*. Pulau Pinang, Malaysia: Institut Masyarakat, 1987.

Ishak Shari, Abdul Samad Abdul Hadi and Abdul Rahman Haji Embong. *Internal Migration Study, Sarawak*. Kuching, Sarawak: State Planning Unit, 1997.

Jensen, Erik. *Money for Rice: The Introduction of Settled Agriculture Based on Cash Crops among the Iban of Sarawak, Malaysia*. Danish Board for Technical Cooperation, 1966.

Jones, Gavin W. "The Thoroughgoing Urbanization of East and Southeast Asia". *Asia Pacific Viewpoint* 38, no. 3 (December 1997): 237–49.

Kibria, N. "Culture, Social Class and Income Control in the Lives of Women Garment Workers in Bangladesh". *Gender and Society*, 9 (1995): 289–309.

Kung, L. *Factory Women in Taiwan*, Ann Arbor, Michigan: UMI Research Press, 1983.

Lee, C. K. *Gender and the South China Miracle: Two Worlds of Factory Women*. Berkeley and Los Angeles: University of California Press, 1998.

Lockard, C. A. *From Kampung to City: A Social History of Kuching Malaysia 1820–1970*. Centre of International Studies, Ohio University, Monographs in International Studies, Southeast Asia Series, no. 75, 1987.

McGee, T. G. "The Emergence of *Desakota* Regions in Asia: Expanding a Hypothesis", in *The Extended Metropolis: Settlement Transition in Asia*, edited by Ginsburg, N., Koppel, B. and McGee, T. G. Honolulu: University of Hawaii Press, 1991.

Morrison, A. "Development in Sarawak in the Colonial Period: A Personal Memoir". In *Development in Sarawak*, edited by Cramb, R. A. and Reece, R. H. W. Australia: Centre of Southeast Asian Studies, Monash University, 1988.

Murray, A. *No Money, No Honey: A Study of Street Traders and Prostitutes in Jakarta*. Singapore: Singapore University Press, 1991.

Ong, A. *Spirits of Resistance and Capitalist Discipline: Factory Women in Malaysia*. New York: University of New York Press, 1987.

Padoch, Christine. *Migration and its alternative among the Iban of Sarawak*. The Hague: Martinus Nijhoff, 1982.

Pringle, Robert. *Rajahs and Rebels*. London: Macmillian, 1970.

Puthucheary, Marvis. "The Planning and Implementation of Agricultural Development in Sarawak: A Case of Centrally Planned Programs. In *Socio-economic Development in Sarawak: Policies and Strategies for the 1990s*, edited by Abdul Majid Mat Salleh, Hatta Solhee and Mohd. Yusof Kasim. Kuching, Sarawak: Angkatan Zaman Mansang (AZAM), 1988.

Ragayah Haji Mat Zin. "Income Distribution and Poverty Eradication in Malaysia: Where do we go from here?". In *Globalization, Culture and Inequalities*, edited by Abdul Rahman Embong. Bangi: Penerbit Universiti Kebangsaan Malaysia, 2004.

Stivens, Maila. *Matriliny and Modernity: Sexual Politics and Social Change in Rural Malaysia*. Australia: Allen and Unwin, 1996.

Sutlive, Vinson. *Development in Sarawak: Myth and Reality*. Paper presented at AZAM Seminar, Kuching, Sarawak, 1984.

Trager, L. *The City Connection: Migration and Family Interdependence in the Philippines*. Ann Arbor: The University of Michigan Press, 1988.

Wolf, D. L. *Factory Daughters: Gender, Household Dynamics, and Rural Industrialization in Java*. Berkeley, Los Angeles, Oxford: University of California Press, 1992.

Yearbook of Statistics Sarawak, 2000 and 2003.

Yeoh, Seng Guan. "Creolized Utopias: Squatter Colonies and the Post-colonial

City in Malaysia". In *Journal of Social Issues in Southeast Asia* (*SOJOURN*) 16, no. 1 (2001): 102–24.

Yeung, Yue-man. "Asia-Pacific Urbanism under Globalization". Paper presented at the 10th Anniversary Conference of the Hong Kong Institute of Asian Pacific Studies, Chinese University of Hong Kong, Hong Kong, 13–15 April 2000.

2

Gender, Wages and Labour Migration

Goy Siew Ching and Low Kuek Long

Introduction

Over the past decades, Malaysia has undergone tremendous socio-economic changes which have had far-reaching consequences on the role and status of women in the country. As a result of these changes, women's participation in the economy, education and labour market has increased. However, women still receive much lower earnings than their male counterparts in the same occupation. It implies that economic development in Malaysia does not foster gender equality. Traditional attitudes about what jobs are suitable and proper for women and that men are the breadwinners of a family are deeply rooted in society. It will therefore take a long time for society to acknowledge the women's subordinate position and attempt to improve it.

In Sarawak, studies on earnings differences between men and women are rare and their results are often not readily available to the public and to women themselves. For this reason, we studied the employment status and earnings of women. This chapter discusses the status of women workers, with special reference to local migrant workers in the manufacturing sector of the Kuching urban labour market. More specifically, the study was designed to examine structures of employment, pattern of labour mobility and a comparison of the earnings of women and men.

Labour Mobility

Labour mobility, is one of the striking features of labour markets. A high degree of labour mobility is due to changes in the general economic conditions, levels of investment in human capital, wage rates, job options and family circumstances. These changes induce workers to change employers, occupations, geographical locations, or a combination of all three. As a result of labour mobility, workers move to the most attractive jobs to eliminate wage differential. The process continues until workers have no incentive to move. At that stage, labour market efficiency is assumed to have been achieved. Labour mobility, however, involves costs. A temporary loss of income can occur between the time one job is given up and a new one is obtained. Furthermore, when geographical mobility occurs, it involves direct moving costs such as transportation cost, psychic costs of leaving family and friends and the familiar job environment, and the loss of seniority and pension benefits. According to the human capital model of mobility, individuals are expected to change jobs or migrate, or both, for their careers if the present value of the gains associated with mobility outweigh the investment costs. In this regard, the human capital model of mobility is a model of "voluntary" mobility undertaken by workers who perceive mobility to be in their self-interest. On the other hand, Acharya and Jose (1991) argued that mobility of workers, that is, job switching, can be both voluntary and involuntary because employment mobility could result in moving up or down the occupational ladder.

About the Study

The data used in this analysis were drawn from the study of Employment, Occupational Mobility and Earnings of Women in the Kuching Urban Labour Market,[1] which was carried out between June 2001 and September 2001. The survey yielded a total of 1,005 respondents of whom 50.6 per cent were female workers. The usual assumption is that only divorced or widowed women seek wage employment outside home. The study, however, indicated that only 2.2 per cent of the female workers were divorced and widowed. An overwhelming majority of the currently employed women were either married (41.5 per cent) or single (56.4 per cent). On the other hand, married men accounted for 62.3 per cent of the sample. The large proportion of single women workers could be due to the nature of the industries covered in the survey. The electrical and electronics industry, which employed 28.5 per cent of the female workers in this study, had a strong preference for single women. This result is consistent with the findings of Lim (1978) and Lee and Sivananthiran (1992, p. 27).

A total of 93.4 per cent of married women workers reported that their husbands were working. It is interesting to note is that almost one third of the wives of married male respondents were working in paid jobs. It is likely that these wives are working because the earnings of their husbands are insufficient to meet the subsistence needs of the family. Married female workers also had fewer children than male workers. The average number of children per married female worker was found to be 2.3 while the male's was 2.5. An overwhelming majority of the respondents had young children below ten years of age.

In terms of years of schooling, female workers had slightly more years of education than male workers (9.99 years against 9.68 years). This difference could be due to a possible bias in favour of women who are engaged in the electrical and electronics industry. According to human resource managers in this industry, the minimum educational requirement for production workers was at least upper secondary.[2] The extent of bias however cannot be determined since the study was confined to a selected number of industries and the location of the survey referred only to the Kuching urban labour market.

In this study, a firm is said to be large if it hires more than 200 workers. If the number of workers is between 50 and 200 it is classified as a medium-sized firm. If the number of workers is fewer than 50, it is defined as a small-sized firm. On this basis, large firms employed 47 per cent of the women and 40 per cent of the men in this study sample. The average employment size of all the establishments surveyed was 282.6 workers with a standard deviation of 607.5. This clearly shows that there is a wide range of employee number among the industries. A detailed look at the average number of employees by industry shows that the electrical and electronics industry (ISIC 38)[3] absorbed an overwhelming majority of the labour force in the Kuching urban labour market. The wood-based industry (ISIC 33) was another important sector in this regard. On the other hand, the food-based industry (ISIC 31) employed an average of 80 workers only per firm.

1. Structure of Employment

The employment distribution is very different between men and women workers. Women tend to be confined in the electrical and electronics industry (28.5 per cent), followed by 26 per cent in the wood-based industry and a further 21 per cent in the food and beverages industry. Men, in contrast, were currently employed mainly in the wood and wood product industries (43.4 per cent), a further 15 per cent in the food and beverages industry, and 13.3 per cent in the electrical and electronics industry.

As a result of rapid economic development, employment opportunities are expanding for women. However, it is important to know whether such expansion leads to diversification into skill-intensive occupational categories which may improve the employment conditions of women. Unfortunately, we found that women only accounted for about 6 per cent in professional and technical-related occupations. The proportion of females in the administrative and managerial category was even lower (5 per cent). In contrast, about 14 per cent of the men were employed in professional, technical-related and managerial categories. About 17 per cent of the women were employed as clerical workers, while less than 5 per cent of the men were employed in this category.

With regards to the distribution of workers by skill level,[4] following the ILO/ARTEP definition (Lee and Sivananthiran 1992, p. 40), it is interesting to note that the proportion of skilled male workers (25.4 per cent) was double that of the females (11.4 per cent). In the semi-skilled level, the percentages of both males and females were more evenly distributed. However, unskilled women production workers outnumbered unskilled men. It explains why women on average earn less than the men and are at the bottom of the employment hierarchy.

2. Pattern of Labour Mobility

2.1 Geographical Mobility

Geographical mobility refers to the movement of workers from one region to another. Of the total 1,005 respondents, 46.3 per cent of the workers originated from outside the Kuching urban labour market. The major geographic sources of migrants into this market were the divisions of Kota Samarahan, Sri Aman and Sibu. Among the migrants, women constituted 47 per cent. Among the female migrants, 47 per cent were Malay, followed by Iban (20.7 per cent), Chinese (14.3 per cent), Bidayuh (12.3 per cent) and others[5] (6 per cent). Among the male migrants, Malay constituted 46.5 per cent, Iban 20.7 per cent, Chinese 14.3 per cent, Bidayuh 11.1 per cent and others 6.6 per cent. These migrants were relatively young. The average age of females at the time of migration was 20.04 years compared with 21.68 years for the males.

Among the 44 per cent of the migrants who were already working prior to migration, women appeared to predominate in the manufacturing sector and other services sectors in comparison to men, who were in manufacturing as well as the forestry and fishing sectors (Table 2.1). It appears that considerable migrants experienced so-called industrial mobility[6] as they moved into the Kuching urban labour market. The wood-based industry attracted a vast majority male migrants while females concentrated in the fabricated, electrical and electronics industry. These workers came in search of better employment opportunities in the Kuching labour market (Table 2.2).

TABLE 2.1
Percentage Distribution of Migrants' Sector of Employment Prior to Migration by Gender

Employment Sector	Male	Female
Agriculture, forestry and fishing	19.0	12.5
Mining	0.8	0.0
Manufacturing	39.7	37.5
Construction	6.6	3.1
Wholesales, retail trade, hotels and restaurant	8.3	9.4
Transport and communication	5.8	1.6
Finance, insurance and real estate	3.3	0.0
Government services	6.6	10.9
Other services	9.9	25.0
Total cases (N)	121	64

TABLE 2.2
Percentage Distribution of the Migrants' Objective to Move by Working Experience

Reason for Migration	Migrants with Working Experience		Migrants without Working Experience		Overall Sample	
	Male	Female	Male	Female	Male	Female
To look for a job	93.4	84.4	69.9	82.4	81.6	82.8
To follow family	3.3	10.9	21.1	12.4	12.3	11.8
To further study	1.7	4.7	8.9	5.3	5.3	5.5
Others	1.7	0.0	0.0	0.0	0.8	0.0
Total cases (N)	121	64	123	157	244	220

For female migrants with working experience before migration another 11 per cent reported that they moved in order to follow their families, bearing in mind that about 43 per cent of them were married prior to migration. Thus family ties often reduce employment and earnings of the migrating wives but increase the employment and earnings of the husbands (Mincer 1978). This phenomenon is clearly reflected in the case of Lily. She is an Iban who worked as an account clerk in a private firm in Miri before migrating to Kuching. Her monthly income was about RM1,000. Two years ago she followed her husband to Kuching where he had a better job offer. Although she secured a clerical job at present in a food manufacturing firm, her salary was slightly below her previous job.

If job changes were the dominant factor motivating geographical mobility among most of the migrants with work experience, then as predicted by human capital theory, we should expect people migrating from areas where wages and employment opportunities are relatively poor to areas where they are relatively good. According to Ronald and Smith (1991), characteristics of the place of origin do not appear to have much influence on migration. Rather people are attracted to the areas where the real earnings of fulltime workers are highest. This has been found to be true in this study. As illustrated in Table 2.3, given the same amount of education and the same length of pre-migration working experience,[7] migrants aged 20–45, earned much less on average before working in Kuching than Kuching-born workers except for migrants with Sixth Form education and above. Through work migration they expected improvement

TABLE 2.3

Mean Monthly Income Comparison between Migrant Status and Educational Attainment

Educational Attainment	Male		Female	
	Kuching	Non-Kuching	Kuching	Non-Kuching
Standard 6 or less	646.57	306.00	283.00	230.00
Form 3	421.82	304.67	399.00	180.00
Form 5	451.23	385.57	408.61	333.43
Form 6	500.00	600.00	400.00	512.00
Diploma and University	822.22	1,325.00	839.47	1,575.00

in income, employment prospects and occupational status. This is what Joyce, a 34-year-old Chinese woman from Sibu had to say:

> I had my first degree from one of the local universities. I started off in Sibu as an auditor in one of the financial institution about ten years ago, earning RM1,600 a month initially. After working there for six-and-a-half years, I resigned. I was unemployed for a few months. I joined the present company in Kuching since December 2000. Now I am the financial administrative manager, earning RM4,000 per month.

As mentioned earlier, geographical mobility incurs costs. Human capital theory clearly predicts that as migration costs increase, the flow of migrants will decline. This suggests that not all workers are equally likely to be involved in geographical mobility.

To be specific, geographical mobility is primarily for the young, single and the better-educated, as human capital theory would suggest. Empirical studies consistently find that age is an important predictor of who will move (Mincer 1978; Lichter 1982; Mulder 1993; Steven 1993). The peak years for mobility among the surveyed migrants with the intention of looking for a job in Kuching were of age 20–24 or 19 and below for both males and females. After the mobility peak during the twenties the percentages of movers decrease with each succeeding age group. The distribution of all movers by age and gender indicates that in the 30–39 age group, the percentage of men engaged in migration decreased drastically to about 11 per cent. For the 40 and above group it was only 4 per cent. The corresponding figures for the women were 4.8 per cent and 1.8 per cent, respectively (Table 2.4). The inverse relationship between age and migration exists because older migrants tend to have higher levels of human capital that are specific to their present employers and losses in terms of psychic cost are larger for older migrants than for younger people. This finding is consistent with the statement by William (1978) that "... many people begin "job shopping" at the end of high school — 18 to 19 — which may result in geographic moves". Consistent with the findings of Mincer (1978), we found that within each age group, unmarried migrants were more likely than married ones to migrate between regions, except for respondents over 29 years of age. Mincer (1978) found that among married people, those without children were more mobile than those with children. Furthermore, among married persons, two-earner households migrated least (Mincer 1978; Litcher 1982; Mulder 1993).

TABLE 2.4

Percentage Distribution of Migrants Marital Status and Age upon Migration

Gender	Age Structure						
	≤ 19	20–24	25–29	30–39	≥ 40	Missing	Total Cases (N)
Male	27.4	39.2	18.8	10.8	3.8	13*	186
Female	49.1	32.1	12.1	4.8	1.8	16*	165
Marital Status							
Married	3.8	20.3	38.9	70.8	66.7	37.9	87
Single	96.2	79.7	61.1	29.2	33.3	62.1	293
Total cases (N)	132	126	55	25	13	29	380

NOTE: * refers to number of cases.

Education plays a very important role in the distribution of individuals over occupational positions in modern societies. It has become very difficult to get a favourable position without the required educational attainments (Blau and Duncan 1967; Hauser and Sewell 1986). The respondents with high educational attainments had a higher propensity to migrate to further their career than did workers with low educational attainment (Table 2.5). Within the 20–24 age group, about two-thirds of the movers had at least upper secondary level of education, while 23 per cent had only primary level of education or less. Our findings reinforced the findings in other countries that younger persons and persons with higher educational attainment migrate more for their careers than older persons or persons with lower educational levels (Markham and Pleck 1986; Mulder 1993 and Greenwood 1975).

Turning to migrants without working experience prior to migration, it was found that a vast majority of the inexperienced migrants entered the manufacturing sector and the wholesale, retail trade, hotels and restaurant sectors when they started their first job in the Kuching market. For this category of migrants, 56 per cent of the women had completed upper secondary level of education compared to 40 per cent of the men. Nevertheless, the average years of education for these migrants were lower than migrants who had working experience prior to migration. On the average, male migrants without working experience had 8.8 years of

TABLE 2.5

Percentage Distribution of Respondents' Educational Attainment and Age upon Migration

Educational Level	Age Structure					
	≤ 19	20–24	25–29	30–39	≥ 40	Total Cases (N)
No formal schooling or less than primary six	7.8 (0.0)	12.3 (3.8)	2.9 (10.0)	11.1 (28.6)	0.0 (0.0)	16 (6)
Primary six	27.5 (18.5)	15.1 (13.2)	25.7 (15.0)	27.8 (42.9)	55.6 (75.0)	44 (31)
Lower secondary	21.6 (18.5)	17.8 (11.3)	17.1 (10.0)	11.1 (14.3)	11.1 (25.0)	33 (25)
Upper secondary	39.2 (61.7)	43.8 (60.4)	40.0 (50.0)	38.9 (14.3)	11.1 (0.0)	74 (93)
Pre-university	2.0 (0.0)	8.2 (7.5)	2.9 (0.0)	0.0 (0.0)	11.1 (0.0)	9 (4)
Diploma	2.0 (0.0)	1.4 (0.0)	2.9 (5.0)	0.0 (0.0)	0.0 (0.0)	3 (1)
University	0.0 (1.0)	1.4 (3.8)	8.6 (10.0)	11.1 (0.0)	11.1 (0.0)	7 (5)
Total cases (N)	51 (81)	73 (53)	35 (20)	18 (7)	9 (4)	186 (165)

NOTE: Figures in parentheses refer to females.

education as compared to 9.2 for male migrants with working experience. Meanwhile, inexperienced women had 9.3 years of education and the experienced ones had 9.6 years of schooling.

2.2 *Occupational Mobility*

As a result of geographical mobility, a migrant experiences a change in his or her occupation or employer. Thus, occupational mobility means a job change. Over half of both male and female migrants experienced job changes. It appears that a greater proportion of women (44.6 per cent) than men (35.6 per cent) have changed employers[8] once during their working life and women had more job changes than men in most of the occupations, except for clerical and production jobs (Table 2.7). Occupational mobility appears to be high among workers who started their working lives in sales and services jobs. Among the women who first started out as sales workers, none of them remained in that occupation although 8.3 per cent of the men did. Similarly, only 3.6 per cent of the women compared with 16.7 per cent of men remained in a services job after a job change. However, fewer female workers (25.3 per cent) changed employers more than twice than did their male counterparts (40.5 per cent). One possible explanation of this higher male workers turnover to some degree is the dual labour market hypothesis that "workers in the secondary segment, consisting of small establishments, tend to display erratic job attachments as a result of poorer working conditions and lower wages" (Lee and Sivananthiran 1992, p. 76). About 48 per cent of the men in small establishments changed employers two or more times compared with 25 per cent of the females.

Nevertheless, the length of stay of respondents in their current job was longer than for their first job, regardless of the number of job changes (Table 2.6). This implies that both males and females used their first job as a stepping stone for employment which offers better terms. This coincides with Acharya and Jose's findings in India that as age, experience and family responsibilities increased, mobility stabilized (1991, p. 47).

Occupational mobility may be up or down the occupational ladder. For instance, 7.1 per cent of the women who first started out as sales workers moved up to professional, scientific and technical jobs, 7.2 per cent moved into clerical jobs, while 57.1 per cent moved down into unskilled production jobs (Table 2.7). Occupational mobility appears lowest

TABLE 2.6

Mean Length of Stay in Each Job in Years by Number of Times Changed Employers

| | Number of Times Changed Employers | | | | | |
| | Once | | Twice | | More than Twice | |
	1st Job	Current	1st Job	Current	1st Job	Current
Male	4.6	5.2	3.5	4.9	2.4	5.5
Female	2.6	4.1	1.5	4.3	1.6	3.3

TABLE 2.7
Percentage Distribution of Workers who Changed Employers at least Once by Their First Job and Present Job by Gender

Present Job	First Job						
	Prof. & Technical Related Workers	Adm. & Managerial Workers	Clerical Workers	Sales Workers	Services Workers	Production Workers	Others*
Prof. & technical related workers	25.0 (14.3)	66.7 (50.0)	8.3 (15.8)	0.0 (7.1)	10.0 (0.0)	0.0 (2.4)	0.0 (0.0)
Adm. & managerial workers	43.8 (14.3)	33.3 (0.0)	16.7 (5.3)	16.7 (0.0)	3.3 (3.6)	5.4 (0.0)	0.0 (0.0)
Clerical workers	0.0 (28.6)	0.0 (50.0)	16.7 (26.3)	0.0 (7.2)	0.0 (7.4)	0.0 (2.4)	0.0 (0.0)
Sales workers	6.3 (0.0)	0.0 (0.0)	8.3 (5.3)	8.3 (0.0)	3.3 (0.0)	3.2 (2.4)	0.0 (0.0)
Services workers	0.0 (0.0)	0.0 (0.0)	0.0 (0.0)	0.0 (7.1)	16.7 (3.6)	6.5 (4.8)	0.0 (0.0)
Skilled workers	18.8 (21.4)	0.0 (0.0)	8.3 (10.5)	25.0 (7.1)	30.0 (3.7)	21.5 (7.1)	14.3 (0.0)
Semi-skilled workers	0.0 (14.3)	0.0 (0.0)	25.0 (0.0)	8.3 (14.3)	16.7 (14.8)	17.2 (23.8)	19.0 (0.0)
Unskilled workers	6.3 (7.1)	0.0 (0.0)	16.7 (36.8)	41.7 (57.1)	20.0 (66.7)	46.2 (57.1)	66.7 (100.0)
Total cases (N)	16 (14)	3 (2)	12 (19)	12 (14)	30 (27)	95 (42)	21 (6)

NOTE: * include construction workers and farmers.
Figures in parentheses refer to females.

among those who began in production jobs. More women (57.1 per cent) than men (46.2 per cent) remained in the unskilled occupational categories. However, 2.4 per cent of the women in unskilled jobs climbed up to professional and related jobs. For instance, Ayu started off as a lowest category technician in one of the publishing companies in Kuching. After few years of working experience, she was promoted to assistant editor in the company. On the other hand 5.4 per cent of the men in unskilled occupational categories moved up to managerial and administrative jobs. Looking at the relationship between a migrant's first job and present job, women (less that 10 per cent) had lower degrees of upward occupational mobility[9] than men (15 per cent). On the contrary, more women (36.6 per cent) moved down the occupational ladder through job changes than men (12.3 per cent), bearing in mind that 25.6 per cent of the women were single during their first job. This indicates that female workers are likely to undertake any kind of job in a factory near their home after marriage in order to carry out their domestic responsibilities. In addition, as mentioned earlier, 11 per cent of experienced working women migrated for the purpose of following their families. Empirical studies show that women are mostly tied movers[10] (Mincer 1978; Bielby and Bielby 1992). They usually have very little ability to initiate a family move for the sake of their own careers. Thus, married women might experience a negative effect on their careers while migration might have a positive effect on the careers of married man.

According to Pratima and Salma (1993), upward mobility can take place even without a job change through promotion in the current establishment. The results show that men in general had a wider scope of moving upward through promotion than women (21.8 per cent of men *versus* 15.5 per cent of women). This is in spite of the fact that women have a marginally higher level of education than men. The results of the logistic regression model[11] indicate that education beyond upper secondary, *ceteris paribus*, has the greatest impact on upward mobility. However, males (probability[12] = 0.406) have better chances to move up the occupational ladder than the females (probability = 0.208).

In terms of the rate of wage gain due to job changes as predicted by human capital theory, the gain in women's wages was relatively small and far less than those of their male counterparts, except for those women who changed jobs only twice (Table 2.8).

TABLE 2.8
Mean Present Monthly Wages by Number of Job Changed

Job Turnover	Male	Rate of Wage Gain	Female	Rate of Wage Gain
Nil	995.22		617.09	
Once	1,521.42	52.9	809.05	31.1
Twice	1,190.58	−22.7	829.95	14.9
> Twice	1,547.53	30.0	876.32	−0.06

3. Gendered Earnings

Earnings in the manufacturing sector differ significantly by gender, with 58.3 per cent of the women earning between RM401 and RM700 per month, whereas only 46.9 per cent of the men earned this amount. In fact, 31.2 per cent of the women earned as little as RM400 per month as compared to only 15.6 per cent of the men. The men's monthly earnings were better spread across different income levels. At the other end of the earning spectrum, the percentage of men earning more than RM1,500 per month was double that of women (Table 2.9). The mean monthly

TABLE 2.9
Percentage Distribution of Monthly Earnings by Gender

Monthly Income Interval (RM)	Male	Female	Total Cases (N)
≤ 300	7.4	8.6	37
301 − 400	8.2	22.6	70
401 − 500	13.5	18.1	73
501 − 600	11.9	17.6	68
601 − 700	11.5	9.0	48
701 − 800	5.7	3.6	22
801 − 1000	7.4	6.3	32
1001 − 1500	11.1	4.1	36
1501 − 2000	4.9	4.1	21
2001 − 2500	3.7	1.4	12
2501 − 3000	4.1	0.9	12
> 3000	10.7	3.6	34
Total cases (N)	244	221	465

earnings of the men (RM1,347.23) far exceeded that of the women (RM754.81).

As expected the mean monthly earnings of workers tend to increase with the level of education (Table 2.10). Even so, it is clear that the average earnings of women are persistently lower than those of men at every educational level. From Table 2.9 above, there were more women than men who received a monthly income below RM600. On the other hand, the gap between women and men widened with increases in the monthly income intervals, with more men earning a higher income. One of the reasons is because women withdraw periodically or even permanently from the job market in order to manage their households, thereby losing experience and seniority. This results in lower earnings for females than for males (Mincer 1978; Mincer and Polachek 1974; Corcoran and Duncan 1979). The biggest disparity is found among those with Sixth Form education. Females earned about 35 per cent that of males.

Differences in educational achievement alone cannot account for all the differences in earnings between male and female workers. Occupational attainment is another factor which could explain the earnings differentials (Table 2.11). As discussed earlier, women tend gravitate to the unskilled categories (56.1 per cent). On the other hand, men tend to have greater access to other occupational categories. This provides evidence that the mean monthly earnings can vary quite widely across occupations. At the upper end of the occupational ladder, the mean monthly earnings of managerial and executive jobs are RM4,886 for men and RM2,809 for women. At the other end of the scale, the mean monthly earnings for unskilled production workers are RM525.1 for men and RM455.8 for women. In terms of earnings, the average monthly earnings of women have been found to be markedly lower than that of the men across all occupational categories, with the exception of the clerical category. A closer examination of the female-male earnings ratios show that they range from a low of 0.34 in the sales workers category to a high of 1.59 in the clerical workers category.

Experience is another factor which affects earnings. Generally, men tend to have longer labour market experience than women. This is important in explaining the mean earning differences between men and women. For female workers who had less than five years of working experience, their mean earnings are about 94 per cent that of the males. For those with five years of working experience, the earnings of women are about 58 per cent that of men. On the other hand, women who have more than ten years of working experience earn about 54 per cent that of men.

TABLE 2.10

Percentage Distribution of Gender Earnings Differentials by Educational Attainment

Monthly Income Interval (RM)	< Standard 6	Standard 6	Form 3	Form 5	Form 6	Diploma	University
≤ 300	10.0 (40.0)	8.8 (15.0)	7.5 (6.9)	7.4 (2.7)	10.0 (25.0)	0.0 (0.0)	0.0 (0.0)
301 – 400	5.0 (33.3)	14.0 (35.0)	10.0 (44.8)	6.3 (15.9)	10.0 (0.0)	3.4 (0.0)	0.0 (0.0)
401 – 500	25.0 (20.0)	26.3 (22.5)	7.5 (20.7)	10.5 (18.6)	0.0 (12.5)	0.0 (0.0)	0.0 (0.0)
501 – 600	5.0 (6.7)	14.0 (12.5)	17.5 (17.2)	11.6 (22.0)	10.0 (25.0)	0.0 (0.0)	7.7 (0.0)
601 – 700	10.0 (0.0)	3.5 (12.5)	25.0 (0.0)	13.7 (11.6)	0.0 (12.5)	11.1 (14.3)	0.0 (0.0)
701 – 800	5.0 (0.0)	8.8 (0.0)	10.0 (0.0)	13.7 (7.1)	0.0 (0.0)	0.0 (0.0)	0.0 (0.0)
801 – 1000	15.0 (0.0)	5.3 (0.0)	5.0 (6.9)	10.5 (9.7)	0.0 (0.0)	0.0 (14.3)	0.0 (7.7)
1001 – 1500	10.0 (0.0)	8.8 (0.0)	10.0 (3.4)	13.7 (5.3)	0.0 (0.0)	33.3 (28.6)	0.0 (7.7)
1501 – 2000	0.0 (0.0)	1.8 (2.5)	2.5 (0.0)	7.4 (5.3)	20.0 (25.0)	0.0 (0.0)	0.0 (0.0)
2001 – 2500	0.0 (0.0)	5.3 (0.0)	5.0 (0.0)	3.2 (0.0)	10.0 (0.0)	0.0 (14.3)	0.0 (22.2)
2501 – 3000	0.0 (0.0)	0.0 (0.0)	2.5 (0.0)	4.2 (0.0)	20.0 (0.0)	22.2 (14.3)	7.7 (11.1)
> 3000	15.0 (0.0)	3.5 (0.0)	2.5 (0.0)	5.3 (0.0)	20.0 (0.0)	33.3 (14.3)	76.9 (66.7)
Total cases (N)	20 (15)	57 (40)	40 (29)	95 (113)	10 (8)	9 (7)	13 (9)
Mean income	1,418.7 (335.9)	825.4 (470.5)	1,096.7 (403.3)	1,091.6 (690.9)	2,124.9 (752.4)	2,411.1 (1,986.4)	4,830.1 (3,437.8)

NOTE: Figures in parentheses refer to females.

TABLE 2.11
Mean Monthly Earnings Differences Across
Occupational Attainment and Gender

Occupational Attainment	Male	Female	Ratio
Professional and technical related workers	3,299.8	2,383.0	0.72
Managerial and administrative workers	4,885.8	2,809.0	0.57
Clerical workers	816.0	1,298.2	1.59
Sales workers	2,276.3	784.2	0.34
Services workers	851.5	386.9	0.45
Skilled workers	1,503.1	1,015.3	0.68
Semi-skilled workers	813.7	680.5	0.85
Unskilled workers	525.1	455.8	0.87

As far as gender earning differentials across industries are concerned, female workers tend to earn substantially lower than male workers. These differences obviously arise primarily because of the concentration of women in lower-paid jobs. The industries where a female worker earns much less than the average (RM754.81) are the beverages industry RM304.7 (40 per cent) and furniture and fixture industry RM427.0 (57 per cent) (Table 2.12).

Table 2.12 also shows that although women generally work longer hours than men in the wood-based, furniture and fixture, and electrical and electronics industries, they earn only 0.59, 0.34 and 0.33 of a male worker's earnings in the respective industries.

Conclusion

A very large proportion of the workers in the manufacturing sector of the Kuching urban market originated from outside the Kuching division. Most of these migrant workers were relatively young and educated. They migrated to Kuching in search of better employment, bearing in mind that 44 per cent of these migrants were already working prior to migration. This carries an important implication that rapid population growth in urban areas through migration will result in serious socio-economic problem on both receiving and sending localities. A more in-depth study of geographical mobility in Sarawak is necessary and useful to ascertain regional development differences and the creation of job opportunities among the various Divisions in Sarawak.

TABLE 2.12

Gender Differences in Earnings by
Selected Characteristics of Industries

Characteristic	Male Respondents		Female Respondents	
Industry	Average Working Hours/Month	Average Monthly Pay	Average Working Hours/Month	Average Monthly Pay
Food	218.0	1,232.0	207.5	594.6
Beverages	197.7	2,260.0	202.7	304.7
Wood products	225.5	951.6	263.6	559.2
Furniture and fixture	230.4	1,257.7	254.8	427.0
Paper products	256.0	545.0	208	1,733.3
Printing and publishing	212.6	1,900.4	207.7	869.1
Non-metallic mineral products	226.9	1,604.2	209.2	569.7
Fabricated metal products	204.6	1,388.3	207.2	939.3
Electrical and electronics products	198.4	2,902.2	222.9	962.1

From our findings, women appear less likely to experience upward occupational mobility than their male counterparts. When they change jobs, they are very likely to move down the occupational ladder. This is because women are often restricted to jobs which are in close proximity to their homes. Female workers also received lower earnings than their male counterparts. Despite the fact that earnings of women increased with the level of education, they still earned less than the men even with the same educational attainments. Furthermore, women were crowded into the semi-skilled and unskilled production categories in the manufacturing sector. A closer look at earning levels by occupational attainments also reveals that women earned less than men even within the same occupational category, with the exception of clerical workers. Therefore, the gender disparity in the Kuching labour market is great.

It is evident from the findings that female participation in the labour market is not enough as most are to be found at the bottom of the work hierarchy. Measures should be taken to enable women to obtain upward mobility in terms of widening their range of occupations, skill content and labour status. As post secondary education contributes significantly to women's earnings, this should be enhanced. Vocational training programmes for school leavers and job seekers should target women. Women should not be sidelined into training programmes which are traditionally perceived as suitable for women but they should be encouraged to enter the fields of science and technology in order to widen their career options. In other words, training programmes offered to women should diversify and include mechantronics (mechanics and electronics), computer studies and others. The private sector can also be motivated to increase women's access to on-the-job training through tax relief. A certain percentage of the Human Resource Development Fund each year should also be allocated for the upgrading of the skills of women in the workplace.

Labour market information is also a key element affecting women's career mobility. The current practice of relying on informal information channels is limiting as women continue to be recruited into highly feminised employment sectors. The Labour Department should step up efforts to disseminate labour market information to young women job seekers and provide labour market counselling.

Child-bearing and family responsibilities often lead women to invest less in human capital formation than men. In order to encourage the continuous participation of women in the labour force, the private sector should provide a more conducive work environment. Childcare facilities, flexitime, career breaks and other flexible workplace practices would ensure that women as a valuable human resource is not lost. State provision of affordable childcare in neighbourhood centres is also vital to support women's labour force participation. Last but not least, both employers and employees perception of what jobs are suitable and proper for women and men must change in order to achieve greater gender equity in the labour market.

Notes

1. The study was funded by the Ministry of Science, Technology and the Environment under the Intensification of Research Priority Areas (IRPA) Cycle 2000.
2. In Malaysia, schooling consists of the following: Primary 1–6, Lower Secondary 1–3 and Upper Secondary 4–5.
3. International standard industry code. Different numbers indicate different types of products.
4. A skilled production worker is someone who has received formal training for at least three months in a specific job or who has more than five years of experience in the given craft. A semi-skilled worker is one who received formal training for a period of two weeks to three months or who had more than one year but less than five years of experience in that particular craft.

Unskilled production workers are those with less than two weeks of training in the job they are performing.

5. It includes Melanau, Lumbawang and Kayan.
6. It refers to workers who change the sector or industry in which they were previously employed.
7. Limited to at most two years of working experience.
8. A change of employer could mean a change in occupation while staying in the same sector or a change in the sector of employment.
9. Occupational mobility groupings adopted in this study were based on the one-digit level. The effect of using one-digit level of classification is that the real extent of occupational mobility may be under-estimated. A three or higher-digit would give a clearer picture of the actual extent of occupational mobility. Therefore, the interpretation of figures concerning upward and downward occupational mobility must be treated with caution.
10. Tied movers are individuals who are disadvantaged in their careers because they migrated with their spouse.
11. $Y = \text{constant} + \alpha LS + \beta US + \delta BUS + \mu$

    where

    Y = a dummy variable which takes a value of '1' if the worker has been promoted at the current firm and '0' otherwise

    LS = a dummy variable which takes a unit value if the worker has completed lower secondary education and '0' otherwise

    US = a dummy variable which takes a unit value if the worker has completed upper secondary education and '0' otherwise

    BUS = a dummy variable which takes a value of '1' if the worker has education beyond upper secondary and '0' otherwise

    μ = error term

Logistic Regression Model

	Male		Female	
	Coefficient	**Odds**	**Coefficient**	**Odds**
Constant	−2.022[a]	0.13	−2.853[a]	0.06
LS	0.668	1.95	0.693	2.00
US	0.881[b]	2.41	1.499[a]	4.48
BUS	1.643[a]	5.17	1.518[a]	4.56
Omnibus test	11.39		8.552	

NOTE: [a] significant at the 1 per cent level.
   [b] significant at the 5 per cent level.
   [c] Ideally, the regression model should be based on occupational categories. The present promoted sample however is too small to permit any meaningful estimates to be made according to the probability of upward mobility based on categories of occupations.

12. The probabilities for male and female workers were calculated as follows: Calculate the Z value. This was obtained by substituting the values of one for US and zero for LS and BS into the estimated logistic regressions for male and female and then summing up with the constant term. The next step was to calculate the probability by using the equation: $P = 1/(1+e^{-z})$.

References

Acharya, S. and A. V. Jose. "Employment and Mobility: A Study Among Workers of Low Income Households in Bombay City". *ARTEP Working Papers*, New Delhi: Asian Regional team for Employment Promotion /International Labour Organization, 1991.

Bielby, W.T. and D. D. Bielby. "I Will Follow Him: Family Ties, Gender-role Beliefs, and Reluctance to Relocate for a Better Job". *American Journal of Sociology* 97 (1992): 1241–67.

Blau, P. M. and Duncan, O. D. *The American Occupational Structure*. New York: Wiley, 1967.

Corcoran, M. and G. J. Duncan. "Work History, Labour Force Attachment, and Earnings Differences Between the Races and Sexes". *Journal of Human Resources* 14 (1979): 1–20.

Greenword, M. J. "Research on Internal Migration in the U.S.: A Survey". *Journal of Economic Literature* 13 (1975).

Hauser, R. M. and W. H. Sewell. "Family Effects in Simple Models of Education, Occupational Status, and Earnings: Findings from the Wisconsin and Kalamazoo Studies". *Journal of Labour Economics* 4 (1986): S83–S115.

Lichter, D. T. "The Migration of Dual Worker Families: Does the Wife's Job Matter?". *Social Science Quarterly* 63 (1982): 48–57.

Lee, K. H. and A. Sivananthiran. *Employment, Occupational Mobility and Earnings in the Kuala Lumpur Urban Labour Market with Special Reference to Women in the Manufacturing Sector*, A Report Submitted to ILO, 1992.

Lim, L. Y. C. "Women Workers in Multinational Corporations: The Case of the Electronics Industry in Malaysia and Singapore". *Michigan Occupational Paper*, no. IX (Fall 1978).

Low, K. L., S. C. Goy, A. L. Jalil and Rosita, S. *Employment, Occupational Mobility and Earnings of Women in the Kuching Urban Labour Market*. Project Sponsored by Intensification of Research in Priority Areas (IRPA), Ministry of Science, Technology and the Environment, IRPA Cycle 2000, 2003.

Markham, W. T. and J. H. Pleck. "Sex and Willingness to Move for Occupational Advancement: Some National Sample Results". *Social Science Quarterly* 27 (1986): 121–43.

Mincer, J. "Family Migration Decisions". *Journal of Political Economy* (1978).

Mincer, J. and S. Polachek. "Family Investments in Human Capital: Earnings of Women". *Journal of Political Economy* 82, pt II (March/April 1974).

Mulder, C. H. *Migration Dynamics: A Life Course Approach*. Amsterdam: Thesis Publishers, 1993.

Pratima, P. M. and C. Z. Salma. *Employment and Occupational Mobility among Women in Manufacturing Industries of Dhaka City: Bangladesh Findings from a Survey of Employees*, Asian Regional Team for Employment Promotion (ARTEP), International Labour Organization (ILO), 1993.

Ronald, G. E. and R. S. Smith. *Modern Labour Economics: Theory and Public Policy*, Harper Collins Publishers, 1991.

Steven R. M. "Employer and Occupational Tenure: 1991 Update". *Monthly Labour Review*, 1993.

William, J. "A Theory of Job Shopping". *Quarterly Journal of Economics* (May 1978): 261–78.

3

Women and Health

Adela Baer

Badong is a poor Melanau village in the Rejang delta near the South China Sea. When I was there, an elderly woman bicycled quietly by on the dirt road raised above the tidal swamp. She wore a frayed sun hat, tattered clothes, and was barefoot. In her bike basket were a few leafy vegetables. She smiled at the sunshine all around her, revealing that she had only four teeth in her pink gums. On the bridge over a tidal creek, a young village man was chatting with me. He sat astride his shiny motorcycle and knew he looked fashionable in his citified "biker" outfit. Does this rural scene personify the old *versus* the new in Sarawak? If so, is there anything wrong with this picture?

This chapter looks at women's health in the kaleidoscope world of Sarawak today. With the rapid transformation of the state, women are beset with both social and cultural forces affecting their health. It is not fanciful that structures such as roads, cities, dams, airstrips, plantations, and resorts impinge on health. Nor must we forget the effects of centralized policies and plans, or of bureaucracies, on people's lives and health in particular. All this is to say that women's health status is far more than the diagnosis and treatment of disease. It is also far more than nutrition, reproduction, and childcare. While reproduction and workloads map closely on health, urbanization and other changes may leave indelible marks. In fact, we must look at women's health embedded in a flux of familiar and alien, close and distant forces. To do so, information from fieldwork is combined with published reports here. This snapshot of women's health can then provide a perspective with some breadth and depth, even though research in this area is sparse.

Many health problems of Sarawak women echo regional situations, according to many reports on illnesses in Southeast Asia. In contrast, the good-health situations in Sarawak seem more homegrown.[1] This is because Sarawak is not as poor as many nation states in the region and once had less gender inequality, economic inequality, or political heavy-handedness.[2] Not having the over-population of Java and being far from a political hotspot have also helped. But in today's interlocked world, Sarawak's advantages are tenuous and its health problems may be growing, despite dedicated efforts to solve them. Not the least reason for a regression is environmental degradation. Inequalities in wealth and education also are substantial. Environmental degradation, lack of wealth, and poor education are especially relevant in terms of women's and children's health in both rural and urban areas. Beyond that, AIDS is a storm front on the horizon.

Despite this somewhat gloomy view, it needs to be said that the health of Sarawak women today is far better than it was a generation ago. For example, the lifespan is increasing and the most dangerous creature in Sarawak, the mosquito, now causes far less malaria than formerly. Also, at first glance in the towns, along the rivers, in the villages, most Sarawakians look healthy. On closer observation, however, ill health becomes more evident. A government midwife has a chronically swollen ankle that she does not know how to cure. An old woman in an Iban longhouse has a conspicuous goitre. A community nurse has numb hands from carpel tunnel syndrome but shuns surgical treatment for fear of medical incompetence. In Lubok Antu town an Iban women tells about a large lump on her breast. A drunk farmer in Sri Aman vomits and, being unable to walk, is shouldered by two women relatives to the afternoon bus to go home. In Bario, a young wife cries while relating how she miscarried when her boss refused to release her from her job to go to hospital in Marudi until she was dangerously ill.

Some would call these "cases" medical problems, but more accurately they are social problems, traditional in some ways and modern in others. This is true because gender inequality on health care has persisted from the colonial into the post-colonial era. Formerly, reproductive health and maternal mortality were taken as the signposts of women's health. Now, however, the universal concept of women's health is more holistic and includes work, sexuality and other aspects of life. The concept also extends to mental health and problems associated with different age groups. Despite this conceptual improvement, little information exists in Sarawak on the diversity of women's experiences of health versus illness other than those related to their reproductive systems.

This lack is especially evident for Sarawak women at different stages of the life cycle. Young women and single women tend to be more at risk of ill health where they have a lower social status than married women do. Mothers have their own set of health issues, especially if they are divorced, abandoned, or single. They may also be held accountable if their children have health-related problems, such as being underweight for their age. Thus, mothers bear the brunt of finger-pointing because fathers are rarely blamed, even though the latter may be spending money on personal consumption rather than on family nutrition. Older women can be the most vulnerable, victims of both sexism and ageism. Social class is also a variable in women's health. Poor women, whether urban slum dwellers or women in remote areas, have difficulty accessing medical services. It is well known that poor women have greater health problems than middle class ones, for obvious reasons.

Survival Data on Women

The maternal mortality rate for Sarawak was higher in the 1990s than for Malaysia as a whole. The figure was 47 per 100,000 live births for Sarawak versus 39 for all of Malaysia. What is most interesting here is that the rate was 92.5 for indigenous groups in West Malaysia plus those in Sarawak and Sabah (East Malaysia), with most of these groups being on the Borneo side. Malays and Indians, and especially Chinese, had much lower maternal mortality rates.[3] Leete and Kwok (1986) earlier reported that Sarawak indigenous women had higher adult mortality than did men over the period 1960–80. Men lived longer than women, one reason being that women did more work. It was not unknown for a Bidayuh man, for instance, to bury two or three wives in succession. Moreover, Grijpstra (1976) showed that among 2,729 Bidayuh, the sex ratio for those over age 59 was 1.28 (55 men to 43 women). The poor survivorship of Bidayuh women was partly due to so-called reproductive depletion (too many pregnancies). Notably, by 1980 the completed fertility of Bidayuh women 40–49 years of age averaged 6.9 ever-born children (Leete and Kwok 1986).[4] However, today with childhood mortality declining and contraceptives widely available for birth spacing, family sizes are becoming smaller.

Some reported sex ratios in Sarawak appear to favour females although they may disregard men working outside the state or "floating" among jobs, but such sex ratios typically have male deficits in the 20–49 age range. In contrast, data that specifically included men working elsewhere gave male-female ratios of 1.17 and 1.13 for Bintulu and Engkari Iban (Padoch 1982). Likewise, the ratio for the Lemanak Oil Palm Scheme was 1.10 (Ayob et al. 1990). These data, like those on maternal mortality, suggest that women survive less well than men in many Sarawak situations. However, the official death rate of all Sarawak women is now lower than for men; in 2000, 4,777 men and 3,497 women over the age of nineteen died.[5]

Over the past century, the health of women has been affected by many social upheavals, from headhunting and slavery to colonial warfare, Japanese domination, and post-war instability. A generation ago, when today's middle-aged women were born, food shortages were common in parts of Sarawak. In the 1970s, 58 per cent of Bidayuh interviewed said their main problem was food insufficiency and another 20 per cent said health was. About 7 per cent of newborns at that time subsequently died (Grijpstra 1976). The diet of pregnant and lactating women was particularly poor (Anderson 1975, 1977).

Largely because of such malnutrition in the past, Sarawak women today are generally small, light-weight people. Iban women average 148 centimetres in height and 49 kilograms in weight. While heights have remained virtually the same for a generation, weights have increased slightly for women. However, older women are a special sub-set. Fortunately, the health of older women, a much neglected topic, received some scrutiny in Song and Kanowit districts. Among Iban women there over forty years of age, their height was about the same as younger women, but they were much thinner, showing chronic energy deficiency in them. This scrawniness was accompanied by sundry ailments and rose in frequency with age.[6]

Factors Affecting Rural Women's Health

1. Outward Migration and Women's Increasing Workload

Good health is the basis for productive work. Many poor rural women in Sarawak work long hours. This has been the case for decades, if not longer.[7] The Bidayuh even have a nickname for a hardworking farm woman. She is called *Birusuk*, meaning that everything she plants grows well (Noeb 1994). Because of farm work, Bidayuh and other villages can look like ghost towns during the day, a point noted earlier by Grijpstra (1976).

Among the rural Selako, women were the breadwinners in a third of the households (Schneider 1978).[8] Only about half of these women-supported families were the result of out-migration by men to live and work elsewhere.[9] Also among the Bau-Lundu Bidayuh, a third of the breadwinners were women (Yaakub et al. 1993). Many were pepper farmers.

In the egalitarian indigenous communities of Sarawak, men and women are complementary and inter-dependent. From the men's point of view, since women are equal partners, much of the farm work can be left to them. It is merely one part of their unpaid family labour. Traditionally, women's farm work was a sociable occupation not regimented to a fixed daily or weekly schedule. Such work can be hot and hard (transplanting rice seedlings into paddies), hot and tedious (weeding hill fields), or strenuous (pounding sago or rice in a mortar).[10] Little work was relaxing (weaving cloth or sleeping mats).[11] Moreover, many Bidayuh farm women walked to their fields, sometimes an hour away. Indeed, they still walk today, often carrying firewood or farm loads. Some spent ninety hours a year transporting such loads on foot (Windle and Cramb 1999).

Many older women stay active and useful as long as possible. Even those over sixty years of age continue to farm to this day; this is the case among the Bidayuh and Kelabit and probably among other groups as well. Older women work slowly but steadily in the fields, as long as they have the ability to trek to and from the countryside. The burden of farm work on both middle-aged and older women is related to the fact that children are now largely in school and many young adults depart for advanced study or employment in the cities. The younger generation is tuned more to Malaysia's insistence on mass culture for its citizens than to traditional lifestyles. Moreover, once children are in school and their mothers accept contraception, such as the pill or tubal ligation, they are then able to work year-round, often in the pepper gardens. In contrast, farming for home consumption once had a slack period of several months for rest and for social gatherings. That period presumably meant less work and more enjoyment for women and their families. The point is that there may be less reproductive depletion but more work depletion for rural women now. In order to avoid this hard work, many younger women migrate to urban areas.[12]

In addition to their productive work in farming, men and children depend on women for their daily needs, such as childcare, domestic chores and nursing the sick — the children, elderly, and men in the family. All these duties place an extra burden on women. In this regard, it is noteworthy that Iban men had more health complaints than the women did in Song and Kanowit (Strickland and Ulijaszek 1992). The healthcare that women provide to their families, both preventive and curative, is largely ignored by officialdom.[13] The time and effort women spend in such care can interfere with their other responsibilities, including farming or wage work. Rarely does the rhetoric of healthcare in Malaysia mention this problem or take it into account in terms of policy decisions.

2. Environmental Degradation

Most people in Sarawak today either live in a village or are connected to the rural world of forest and field by family ties or recent memories. About 80 per cent of Sarawak land was once rainforest, containing a wealth of animal and plant life that sustained human culture and existence. But no longer. Politicians' lofty pronouncements about preserving the forest and biodiversity have not prevented some from becoming wealthy from timber extraction in Sarawak (Colchester 1989).

Commercial destruction of natural resources impacts women's lives and health. Logging can kill more trees than loggers harvest, and it seriously erodes soils, causes silting, and precipitates flash flooding (WWF Malaysia 1985). Aquatic resources of fish, snails, and turtles suffer greatly, not only from turbidity but from diesel oil pollution. Deer and wild pigs, traditional sources of necessary protein, are now extinct over wide areas. Cash earned from the sale of gathered illipe nuts, resins, herbs, and bamboo has declined; such gathering no longer functions as a fall-back source of rural cash for buying necessities.

While women do not incur chainsaw accidents in the logging industry as men do, women seem to bear the brunt of its many ill effects on health, either directly or in terms of their children. In traditional areas, women collected ferns and other wild foods in forests and fallows, at least weekly (Hew and Kedit 1987). In un-deforested Nanga Sumpa in the 1990s, 103 edible wild plant species were being foraged by Iban, while in Kelabit country, at Pa Dalih, 68 wild species were foraged (Christensen 2002). In both cases, the menu for meals was far more varied than anything a city restaurant can offer. Hence, diminishing food variety as a result of deforestation has serious health implications.

Chemical treatments of villages or farm areas are now common in rural areas (Burgers et al. 1991) and have health implications. Besides their cost, they present ecological problems. For example, fishing declined in Singai as herbicides became widely used in pepper or cocoa plots.[14] Run-off from oil palm plantations also kills fish in Melanau areas. Such chemicals also present health problems to humans. Effluents from oil palm processing plants have made some major rivers unusable for drinking or bathing (Colchester 1989). Recently the herbicide called Roundup was apparently applied topically in Bario, in a foolish attempt to cure scabies there. Also, in the past DDT has been used for decades to ward off mosquitoes. It persists in the soil and can become toxically concentrated (through the food chain) in hen's eggs and breast milk. DDT is a health hazard that will not disappear for many years in Sarawak.

Many villages now have tap water, which frees women from hauling water home every day. But the tap sometimes dries up. This means the women have to go back to traditional methods of water collection from springs, rivers, or swamps, even if they are unhealthy sources of water. In Serikin, Bau district, urban visitors complained they could not take a bath when the tap ran dry, but the difficulty of getting water for other household use was not commented on (Yaakub et al. 1993).

Another major environmental change which has occurred in the rural areas is the construction of hydroelectric dams. There are two hydroelectric dams in Sarawak. The first is the Batang Ai dam in the Sri Aman division and the more recent Bakun dam in the upper Rejang River basin. The account below provides a view on unsettling living conditions resulting from the Bakun dam construction project, including health implications.

The statement of an anonymous woman resettled in Asap due to the Bakun project:[15]

I want to return to my old home. Let the authorities be enraged, I can't be bothered. I have no money here, the fish are all gone, the vegetables finished...The price of the house is unreasonable. Even the stairs are damaged already. In my old home the quality of our houses was so much higher. We had cement floors. I used to weave mats in my old home for sale. Now I can't even find rattan.

Everyone has bills here. Move an inch, you have to pay for something. Before, we could sell our fish and save the money for the few bills that we had to pay. Now, I need at least RM10 to take my ailing mother to the clinic. She has been lying here, unable to rise for three days already. We can't even celebrate our festivities here. Even the betelnut and sirih would have to be paid for. We need to walk for an hour to go to the nearest shop. Doesn't the government care?

All my children have stopped going to school because we can't afford it. We need to buy rice. Sometimes, we have to borrow it. Look at my grandniece, she is so thin now. Back home, even if you are sick, food is abundant.

These days we can't even sleep well. The men have been drinking a lot and they create a commotion when they are drunk at night. There's banging on the walls and all. There have been accidents caused by drunk driving. I don't want to make more tuak [wine]. The men have been drinking excessively. The women too. [Silence] Do you have RM50 to spare me? My mother's sick. She needs to go to the clinic.

Common Health Problems in Sarawak

1. Rural Health Issues

(i)   *Undernutrition and Malnutrition*

Strickland (1986) estimated that Tebakang Bidayuh men were eating 2,000 kcal per day and the women were eating 1,700 kcal in the 1970s, neither amount being adequate to cope with an active life. A Kenyah rule of thumb was that four men would eat the same amount of rice as five women (Chin 1985). More recently, twenty-seven Sarawak Dayak women were studied for food intake versus energy expenditure (Ismail et al. 2002). They took in 6.6 energy units daily and expended 8.1 units. They were in "negative energy balance," that is, not eating enough to sustain them. They had a food deficit of 20 per cent. The twenty-four Dayak men surveyed were eating 9.3 energy units and expending 9.1, thus being energy-balanced. They were also eating 40 per cent more energy food than the women were.

With Malaysian culture now emphasizing a cash economy, buying food has become the norm. A family's options about food are limited. It can produce enough food to sustain itself, buy food to achieve that end, or become malnourished. Many factors enter into this situation, such as government policies, the timber industry, agro business, world market forces, family cash-cropping, and off-farm employment. Often food security is lost in this welter of factors.

Fewer types of food crops are now grown or consumed and, in fact, diets are generally more restricted than formerly. According to Gerrits (1994), Bidayuh in Gayu village grew thirty-four species of secondary crops in their swidden fields, with vegetable intercropping being common. In spite of this, Grijpstra (1976) reported a generation ago that few Bidayuh had kitchen gardens to provide green vegetables year-round. This is still the case in many Bidayuh, Melanau and other areas. In other words, even if inter-cropping was common throughout rural Sarawak, it provided nutritious vegetables for home consumption just for part of the year. Only when people had access to fallow fields and forests were they able to forage for food and medicinal plants year-round. With deforestation and giant plantation schemes, this is no longer the case in many areas.

In fact, villages seem to have more ornamental plants by their houses than edible greenery. The resulting paucity of vegetables in the diet puts extra stress on those already malnourished, including women. Fruit trees are still found in many, but not all areas. Although fruits such as durian may be grown for sale, smaller fruits tend to be for home consumption. Some longhouses have been encouraged to remove shading fruit trees, to make the compound "look tidier" (Alexander and Alexander 1993), but this urban view of aesthetics ignores the health benefits of both fruit and cooling shade for living quarters.

Fish and meat consumption now is problematic without cash in hand. As mentioned previously, rivers are less productive for several reasons and game animals are scarce, largely because of logging and giant plantations of export crops. Domestic animals kept for food are not abundant throughout rural Sarawak. Even then, they may be sold rather than eaten. One malnourished Melanau woman has long kept a few ducks. She often sells the eggs but has never tasted duck meat or the eggs. However, Iban in "suburban" Bawang Assan near Sibu now eat more meat than previously was the case (Edwards 2000).

In some villages fish ponds were encouraged. Later, many were dry holes, the fish gone, whether dead, eaten, or sold. If such a pond were connected to an animal pen and a vegetable garden nearby, the integrated system would have been more productive and sustainable. In Laos, for example, "the animal manure fertilizes the garden and feeds the fish, and water from the pond irrigates the garden" (Ireson 1996, p. 249).

For many rural women then, an adequate and balanced diet eludes them today. While there are many causes of this food deficiency, it has received far too little attention by the government. One way to ameliorate this problem, at least in some areas, is to encourage kitchen or neighbourhood communal gardens and provide vegetable seeds on demand (Alexander and Alexander 1993).

(ii) *Goitre*

Goitre has been common in many inland areas of Sarawak for generations, probably centuries. It is caused by a lack of iodine in the diet. Coastal people seldom have goitres because the seafood they eat contains iodine. Many inland people have goitres because they eat little seafood and their physical environment provides little iodine. In addition, poor people eat both the leaves and tubers of cassava, a plant that contains goitrogens. These compounds snatch iodine from its needed role in the thyroid gland.[16] The inland Kelabit, however, were once largely goitre-free because their salt supply came from iodine-rich water laboriously evaporated at local springs. Groups in the Baram such as Kayan and Kenyah once traded for this iodized salt from the Kelabit Highlands (Sellato 1993).

Women are more prone to goitre than men. Women lose iodine from the body when they provide it to their offspring during pregnancy.[17] In the 1960s, 39 per cent of 1,750 women throughout Sarawak had visible goitres (Polunin 1971). In the Rejang region in 1970, 33 per cent of Iban females and 8 per cent of males were goiterous (Ogihara et al. 1972*a, b*). Goitre increased from age 10 up to age 60 and then the prevalence levelled off, with older people having larger goitres. Likewise in the 1970s, in the uplands of the Ai River basin, 99 per cent of the population had goitres (Maberly and Eastman 1976). In the 1980s, in the Tinjar area of the Baram, 78 per cent of the women studied (largely Kenyah, Kayan, and Iban) had palpable goitres (Chen and Lim 1982). As late as 1993 in Lubok Antu District, 75 per cent of women in the Ai area and 49 per cent of them in the Lemanak area had goitres (Foo et al. 1994 and 1996). This was the case in spite of the fact that iodized salt had been freely distributed by health workers to this district for decades. To counteract this situation, iodine was then introduced into the piped water supply of selected villages by the rural health service. Within one year, the goitre prevalence there dropped from a range of 49 to 83 per cent down to a range of 26 to 47 per cent. By late 1997, 300 Sarawak villages and 40 government boarding schools had been provided with an iodinated water supply (Kiyu et al. 1998). In addition, iodized salt continues to be distributed free to villages that need it. While goitre is now on the wane, its previous high level in women may help explain why thyroid cancer is almost twice as common in women as men (Kiyu 1985).

(iii) *Anemia*

Anemia, or blood poor in hemoglobin, is largely due to a lack of iron and folate in the diet. Anemia drains strength and energy, especially from women who lose blood through menstruation and delivery. This loss is in addition to nurturing the blood supply of their offspring during pregnancy.

In rural West Malaysia, 25 per cent of women 18–60 years of age in a large study were anemic, making them the most anemic group there (Khor 2002). Children up to the age of 13 and the elderly were not far behind, with 24 per cent and 23 per cent, respectively. Men 18–60 had the lowest anemia prevalence, under 14 per cent.

In Sarawak, anemia was recently studied in five ethnic groups in the remote Rejang uplands (Sagin et al. 2002b), but the results are not comparable to those for West Malaysia. While 38 per cent of Rejang adults over 60 years of age were anemic, *versus* 23 per cent in West Malaysia, elderly women were poorly represented in the Sarawak sample. In fact, few Rejang females over the age of 40 were studied, possibly because older women did not survive as well as older men there. Among the five ethnic groups studied, there were no women who had reached 70 years of age, but quite a few men in their 70s and 80s. Given this caveat, it is difficult to interpret the study's finding that 29 per cent of all the males studied but only 17 per cent of the females were anemic, an unusual finding for Sarawak. One factor appears to be that pregnant and lactating women were included in the sample. Since only 12 per cent of the females aged 31–40 years were anemic while 23 per cent of the males were, many women were likely receiving iron-folate supplements to prevent a rash of anemia in them. In contrast, it is significant that 32 per cent of females 11–20 years of age were anemic but only 4 per cent of the males in this age cohort were.

Indeed, Strickland and Duffield (1997) found 47 per cent of non-pregnant Iban women were anemic (defined as hemoglobin less than 12 g/dl) compared to 40 per cent of the men (Hb<13 g/dl). Severe anemia (Hb<9 g/dl) was reported for 3.4 per cent of pregnant women in Sarawak in 1994, despite the widespread availability of iron-folate supplements for them (Duffield and Strickland 1999). Moreover, Tee and colleagues (1999) found that 44 per cent of girls 12 to 17 years of age studied in Samarahan district were anemic, with 19 per cent being severely or moderately anemic (Hb<12) and the rest borderline anemic (Hb 12–13). After providing twenty-two weeks of treatment with iron-folate supplements, the average haemoglobin level was over 13 g/dl. That is, very few of the 1,408 girls studied were still anemic.

Anemia in pregnant women is a major factor leading to fetal loss or low birth weight (LBW) in offspring. Mothers in Lundu Hospital with anemia, haemorrhage, hypertension, or pre-eclampsia had four times more LBW children than mothers without these conditions, that is, 45 per cent versus 10 per cent LBW offspring (Yadav 1994). As is well known, LBW is the main cause of deficiencies in infant growth and survival worldwide.

(iv) *Intestinal parasites — worms*

Few studies exist on intestinal parasites in Sarawak women. Often such studies are confined to children, since they are known to have infestations. However, Sagin and colleagues (2002*a*) studied this problem in women in the upper Rejang area. They found that the infection rate was higher in women than in men, and almost the same as in children. While 57 per cent of the women were infected, 66 per cent of the children were infected, but only a third of the men were. The researchers suggested that women were infected because they were in daily contact with children's faeces, given that transmission is commonly from child to child by the fecal-oral route and then from child to mother.[18] Where children defecate indiscriminately and put contaminated hands (or anything hand-held) into their mouths, transmission is continuous unless long-term treatment is provided.

Most infected women in this study had Trichuris worms, but a few had roundworms or hookworms. The health effects of these worms include anemia, fatigue, dysentery, and a weakened immune system. Geddes noted that a gloomy girl became much gayer "after she had been given a dose of particularly effective worm medicine" (1954*b*, p. 39). Treating all children and adults with antihelminthics would interrupt the sequence of poor fetal growth, low birth weight, and childhood stunting.

(v) *Teeth*

Poor teeth are another sign warning of malnutrition. This is especially obvious in older, toothless people. Indeed, toothless elders seem to be endemic in rural Sarawak. According to one Malaysian report, 47 per cent of elderly people surveyed had difficulty in chewing food (Sushama 1992). A generation ago, Oldrey lamented the dreadful state of dental health in the Punan Busong: all but small children had gross decay and many teeth "had crumbled away to gum level, leaving a few discolored stumps" (1972, p. 275).

Dentists are rather rare in Sarawak, with one for about every 26,000 people (Wong 1992). Most are private practitioners in urban centres who are not visited by poor people because of high fees or transport costs. Most of the twenty-six government dental clinics are also in towns and cities, and while they have low fees, they are understaffed.

People once brushed their teeth with homemade toothbrushes. Some Bidayuh used a sliver of coconut shell full of bristles (Calder 1954). Iban used *biansu* twigs. How effective these were in preventing tooth decay is unknown, but Lahanan adults and children brush their teeth regularly and yet suffer frequent toothaches (Alexander and Alexander 1993). They over-consume aspirin or panadol for pain relief. While a local paramedic extracts teeth, restorative treatment by a dentist is virtually unavailable. The craving for sweets (store-bought) in an otherwise non-sweet rural diet is also part of the problem.

2. Urban Health Issues

Few studies exist on the health status of the urban population in Sarawak. Although sexually transmitted diseases are addressed in this section, these diseases respect no boundaries. They are discussed here because they are more prevalent in the cities than in the rural areas.

(i)   *Sexually Transmitted Diseases (STDs)*

STDs with the most serious consequences for women include syphilis, gonorrhea, and the HIV viral infection that leads to AIDS. Sarawak has the highest rate of reported STDs in Malaysia. The state also has a low level of safe-sex practices (Rintos 2001; Chong 1999). Sarawak recently had 2,500 new STD cases reported annually.[19] In 2001, about 40 per cent of all reported STD cases in Sarawak were syphilis, 60 per cent were gonorrhea and less than 1 per cent were HIV/AIDS.[20] While STDs occur in all sectors of the Malaysian population, their significance is particularly acute in the sex industry.

In the following scenario, a profile of the sex industry for women is given, based on information from West Malaysia (Nagaraj and Yahya 1998). For lack of general information on female sex workers in East Malaysia, it can only be suggested that the situation in Sarawak is similar.[21] Nevertheless, STDs are a well-known risk for sex workers in many parts of the world.

Malaysian Female Sex Workers and Health: A Scenario

It is said that every town and city in Malaysia has a sex sector, perhaps every hotel and karaoke lounge. This is a lucrative "business" for Malaysia, for its crime syndicates, and for pimps. While it exploits females in many ways, it is relatively well-paying for poorly educated girls and for women who do not have children, even though many of them must remit money to their parents' home. It also attracts a few women who are prone to conspicuous consumption. Although sex workers generally lack the skills to work in a factory or office, they can earn far more than in those daytime jobs. A brothel worker can net RM70 per customer. With as few as fifty customers per month, this provides a monthly income of RM3,500.

The health consequences of this work are various. Sex workers can be poorly informed about STDs. Some think, erroneously, that a medical check-up will prevent or cure an HIV infection. Yet to their credit, many insist that their customers use condoms. Many also go for medical check-ups, usually to private clinics. Those who have contracted STDs have paid for their treatment. Some have reported having had an abortion. Not a few are single mothers.

Since sex work is not regulated in Malaysia, no effective way exists to control the spread of STDs *via* this business sector — especially to control the spread through the customers to their other sexual partners. It is time to be practical about commercial sex and STDs in Malaysia, rather than moralizing about them. In the short term, the best way to end exploitation and oppression of female sex workers is to legalize and regulate the sex trade, including laws mandating appropriate public health measures and laws curbing associated criminal organizations. This would not only dampen the spread of AIDS, it would remove the lucrative economic benefits to pimps and syndicates and cut down on vice crime in general. In the long term, however, the best way to end exploitation of these women is to ensure all women receive respect and job opportunities equal to those of men. Time is running out.

Gonorrhea is a disease for which there is no vaccine and no long-term cure for sexually active people. Once infected, people can pass the disease on for several months. After this period, they become susceptible to reinfection. For this reason the disease can persist even in small, scattered populations in Sarawak. Although it might seem a paradox, gonorrhea can impact women greatly, even though many women have no symptoms. Men are more likely to have symptoms, and when they do, they can obtain antibiotic treatment that clears the current infection. But for women, gonorrhea can produce pelvic inflammatory disease, which is a leading cause of sterility and associated ectopic pregnancy. If this is a problem in Sarawak, it has not been well studied, despite concerns about sterility in some ethnic groups in the past.

In the 1950s UN workers in Sarawak reported on a deputation of Iban women who trekked to Kuching to urge the Medical Department to tackle the sterility that was making inroads among the Iban:

> Instead of practicing fertility rites and regarding their declining fertility as a visitation by the gods, the women recognized that the doctors could do something about it. And they probably can, because the epidemic of sterility is most likely due to the spread of venereal diseases... (Calder 1954, p. 48)

In the past, and continuing today, some Sarawak men work for months or years away from their families. The more they are away from home, the more likely they are to contract STDs. When, or if, the men do return home, their wives are then vulnerable to STD transmission. It seems that gonorrhea was quite common in Sarawak in the past. De Zulueta (1957) believed that the population of the upper Tinjar (largely Kenyah) was dying out due to the high incidence of gonorrhea there. Gonorrhea may also have contributed to the high sterility attributed to Iban women in the 1960s.[22] Thus, STDs are carried from the urban to the rural areas of Sarawak. Today gonorrhea is the most common STD reported in Sarawak. In addition, gonorrhea helps spread AIDS.

(ii) *AIDS*

In biological terms the HIV virus causes AIDS, but AIDS is a growing epidemic in Southeast Asia largely for other reasons. Knowledge about AIDS and about safe-sex practices is woefully inadequate in Sarawak (Rabi'al and Kiyu 1995). Beyond that, knowledge itself is of little practical value if attitudes are unrealistic about ways to prevent AIDS.

There has been no mass screening for the HIV virus in Malaysia, only screening of selective high-risk groups, such as injecting drug users who may share hypodermic needles. Based on these studies, HIV/AIDS rates are rising in Malaysia as a whole, with 853 reported AIDS cases in 1990 *versus* 4,942 in 1992 (Lye et al. 1994). By 1998, 24,000 infections were known officially, mostly in men, but a better estimate is 60,000 (Rokiah Ismail 1998). By 2001, there were 40,049 known infections with some 4,000 deaths.[23] By mid-2004, 58,000 HIV infections were estimated to exist (*Bernama* 2004), of which 5.5 per cent were in women. In Sarawak, however, 20 per cent were in women (*Bernama* 2003).

In Sarawak, most HIV infections are largely due to heterosexual transmission, rather than bisexual or homosexual transmission, or to any association with drug addiction. This means that women in Sarawak are more vulnerable to HIV infections than those in West Malaysia. Unfortunately, the research literature is largely silent on AIDS/HIV in Sarawak women. A relevant report comes from Kelantan where Wai and colleagues (1996), tested 171 women for HIV and syphilis at the only drug-rehabilitation centre for women in Malaysia. Some of the women had acquired HIV by sharing needles during drug usage, but 48 per cent of them had been sex workers. Moreover, 60 per cent of these women said their sexual partners never used condoms. This is significant because condoms are readily available in Malaysia (which, in fact, manufactures them). Since HIV is more often transmitted to women sex workers by male clients than the other way around, it comes as no surprise that 14 per cent of the 171 women were found to be HIV-positive. Even more of the women tested positive for syphilis — 39 per cent. However, sex work was not correlated with the presence of HIV in the Kelantan study, although sharing drug needles was. This would not be the expectation for Sarawak. In Sarawak, prostitution is all too common but glue sniffing rather than intravenously injecting opiates is the usual Sarawak drug behaviour. For Sarawak, then, one would expect HIV in women to be correlated with sex work and, increasingly, for HIV infection to become common in wives whose husbands were customers of sex workers or were generally promiscuous. Already in Sarawak, couples make up 30 per cent of the HIV cases (Chong 1999). This home-based transmission clearly victimizes women.[24]

Since major HIV epidemics tend to occur in areas where unprotected sex is common in heterosexual contacts (Jha et al. 2001), all men and women who have multiple sex partners are the core group to be addressed to stop the spread of HIV and other STDs. While condoms do not protect against some STDs, their use by this core group can cheaply and efficiently minimize HIV transmission *via* heterosexuality.[25]

By the year 2000, Sarawak had 185 test-positive HIV carriers, with the majority estimated to be due to heterosexual contacts. By mid-2001, Sarawak had 309 reported HIV carriers, of whom forty had died of AIDS, suggesting that the number of infections rose dramatically in one year. By mid-2004, the state had 424 reported carriers, but the number of deaths was not mentioned (*Bernama* 2004). The rate of new infections may now be exploding in Sarawak, just as it is doing in Indonesia (Cohen 2001).

Health workers have publicized the threat of AIDS to some extent. In Lundu district, nurses have given talks to village women about AIDS, but the women have pointed out that the talks should be given to the men, as they are the ones who bring it in from outside. The women "just stay at home", they said.[26] These women realized they could be put at risk, not because of their own sexual behaviour but their partner's. To their credit, the health workers then decided to give these talks to the men at a later date.

Medical Services

Many government health services in Sarawak are accepted and appreciated by its citizens. For example, childhood immunizations are widespread and have obviously cut down on illnesses and deaths that formerly victimized families or whole communities. The development of a road system over the decades has also provided better access and usage of clinics and hospitals to people living in remote locations (Windle and Cramb 1999). As for health facilities and personnel, they have increased in number throughout the past half century (Chew 1994; Sarawak Government 1997). For example, mobile health teams and the "flying doctor" service regularly visit the Penan, bringing "joy and delight" to them; their sick are treated and medicines are dispensed free of charge (Hatta Solhee and Langub 1993, p. 244).

In spite of a good network of health facilities throughout the state, they are under-utilized. For instance, pap smears are available in Malaysia, but Rashidah (1999) reported that only 25 per cent of women studied had had a pap smear, with rural, poorly educated, and single women especially under-served. While the medical profession often views women as ignorant, especially poor or rural women, many reasons exist for women to be ambivalent about health services. First, these services for women in Sarawak are overly focused on maternal and childcare, home economics style nutrition, and fertility control. Generally, women staffers supervise these matters, but male medical staff handle other types of problems. In other words, while women are major consumers of health services, they are often exposed to a male-dominated health profession. This is compounded in the higher medical ranks, where most specialists are men. The more serious a woman's ailment, the more likely she will be treated by a male doctor. Women are therefore most vulnerable when dealing with the most powerful members of the medical profession. In addition, in multi-ethnic Sarawak, people often are treated by professionals from a different ethnic group who do not speak their language or understand their culture.[27] Thus women's powerlessness is compounded not just by gender, but by social class, language and culture when they use state services.

The lack of privacy in institutional settings and during medical exams further discourages women from seeking state health care in Sarawak. Thus, their attendance records at clinics and hospitals may underestimate their health problems, reflecting a reluctance to attend. In official discourse on women's health, gender sensitivity is often replaced by a highly medicalized perspective where women are blamed for their problems. In addition, they fear being shut away in a hospital under the control of strangers who perform incomprehensible procedures on them. In one case, a Melanau woman with a high risk of birth complications absconded from the Mukah hospital in the middle of the night with something uneasy on her mind. She made it back to her home in Oya and, by sheer luck, had a normal delivery there.

Another reason why Sarawak women say they do not go to a medical facility is that they do not think they are sick, or they have no spare time for going, or they have no one to take care of their children if they are away. Some women do not like the reception they receive at medical facilities. Some lack transportation money when they are referred to faraway hospitals, especially if several visits are required for a series of tests and treatments. Others have little confidence in modern medicine.[28] As a result, women often turn to self-medication or to family and friends to deal with their health problems. Yet little is known about how Sarawak women try to solve these problems because research has largely neglected this area. Likewise, little is known about the difference between how women view their health problems and how the government views their problems. Assuming women's values and bureaucratic values differ, it would be useful for officials to pay more attention to the health situation of women by listening instead of declaiming.

Thus, in view of the many disadvantages that indigenous women in Sarawak face, the "Kuching Statement on the Health of Indigenous Peoples" was adopted at a world conference on health, held in Malaysia in 1999. It affirmed the need for health professionals to receive training in indigenous health issues and to adequately address the health of indigenous women in particular (Kamil and Teng 2002).

Health Education

Health education is virtually a top-down exercise in Sarawak as in many other places. Officials decide what advice to give out and usually assume it will be correctly understood and acted upon. They are little concerned with the people's views. When Bidayuh household heads were asked about their problems, they named rice insufficiency, shortages of cash and health problems (Grijpstra 1976). It is striking that wives were not consulted on these matters.[29] Instead, the wives were subjected to a "home economics extension" survey (Anderson 1975).[30] It covered their kitchen facilities, methods of food storage and refuse disposal, house design, furniture, house and compound cleaning schedule, quantity of flowers planted by the house, and similar subjects. Although the women were not asked directly about health, virtually all of them listed food as their commonest purchase when cash was available. Over 80 per cent of them listed rice, meat, poultry, eggs, fish, milk, vegetables, Milo, fruits and beans as being nutritious foods. Only a minority (30 per cent) thought soda drinks or alcohol were nutritious.

Some men may not be aware of nutritional values. Recently, a university student group studied malnutrition in a Bidayuh village near Tebedu and reported their findings and advice to the village development committee. The fifteen or so committee members, all men, heard the students out, thanked them, and said they would work on the students' proposals. One observer surmised that the men were thinking: "Of course the kids are skinny, so were we when we were their age. Why are these young outsiders making such a fuss?" Some men are even said to think that malnutrition only refers to the plight of the starving Africans that they see on television!

Grijpstra noted that home demonstrators from the Department of Agriculture visited rural villages to teach women "how to grow vegetables, new methods of cooking, hygienic measures, etc." (1976, p. 149). This had little impact on the health of the women or of their families because the women had little time or energy for these extra tasks. In addition, women are farmers and cannot be relegated solely to the domestic domain. Often male farmers receive information on the use of toxic pesticides but women may be the ones using these chemicals in the field. Had the government workers asked the women what their needs were for improving health, more could have been accomplished.

Today many medical clinic walls are plastered with publicity posters about health and illness. Since not a few rural, indigenous women are functionally illiterate, the fact that a poster is in Malay rather than their own language does not matter to them.[31] When it comes to women's films on health, however, problems can multiply, as noted in Sarawak's neighbouring state of Sabah:

> Many of the Murut women…were unfamiliar with [Malay], particularly at the level of sophistication used in this film. The film depicted urban, middle-class women with very Western lifestyles. Indeed, some time was devoted to the issue of combining childcare and breastfeeding for professional women. The [Murut] women…would never have encountered this situation…Many of the issues raised in the breastfeeding film…bore no relation to the experiences of the audience. (Chandler 1989, p. 120)

If women received better health information, the number who think that leprosy is caused by "wrong" foods, weakness, or "dirty" blood, would decline. Those who attribute serious illness to demons would be able to reconsider their outlook. Those who think malaria results from eating too much sugarcane might become aware of mosquito transmission. And maladaptive food taboos during and after pregnancy might also decline.

Curiously, while Sarawak women are encouraged to breastfeed their infants, urban views on female modesty have led some women to forego breastfeeding because they encountered bare-breast taboos earlier at a government boarding school (Alexander and Alexander 1993).

Conclusion

Malaysia is a country committed to achieving the status of an industrialized, developed nation. Since Sarawak joined Malaysia in 1963, the state has intervened in local society and culture, far more than earlier regimes. This has produced far-reaching socio-economic and environmental changes. The consequences of these for women's health have been poorly understood or appreciated, even today.

Urbanization itself highlights health issues that overlap or differ between rural and urban women. However, on the socio-economic front, both working and living conditions are more onerous for rural women. They are, in the main, less educated and less prosperous than their urban sisters. In addition, environmental degradation and pollution add to the burdens of rural women.

On a broader scale, health services can be institutionally blind to the fact that poor women's health is associated with poverty. Furnishing pregnant women with multi-vitamin tablets is a stop-gap measure. Many health problems cannot be solved piecemeal or by a quick-fix. Long-term benefits would accrue if women had the same job opportunities as men and received equal pay for wage work with men. Officially approved women's income generating projects, such as basket weaving for the fickle tourist trade, do not alleviate women's poverty. Such "development" projects marginalize women further while treating their problems superficially.

It must be said that the health services in Sarawak generally respond well to acute problems. Chronic problems, however, may require more information being made available, more time and more money spent in order to provide and maintain a state of health. Under-nutrition is a prime example of a chronic problem for many women and children. Although medical people often collect data on its extent and severity, at least for children, such data do not in themselves reveal the decisions and actions needed to solve the problem (Pellitier 1992). People living in poverty may not be aware of the insidious effects of under-nutrition and may not solve this problem for many reasons. For example, they may face other more immediate problems that loom larger, such as a leaky roof or a dry water pipe. At the same time, frontline health workers who recognize the problem cannot solve it solely in the context of medical information and policies. Both groups are boxed in. Compartmentalization is therefore counter-productive. This issue requires thoughtful coordination of agency to agency, of government to its citizens, of men and women.

Sarawak is changing in diverse ways, some of which foster women's health while others do not. Women's views need to be listened to, their health status outside pregnancy studied, their living and working environment improved. In the final analysis, the key to improving women's health is in improving women's position in society and this, ultimately, is Sarawak's challenge.

Notes

1. For example, Sarawak's maternal death rate in the 1990s was only 7 per cent of that in Laos, that is, 47 *versus* 653 deaths per 100,000 live births (Ireson-Doolittle and Moreno-Black 2003).
2. See, for example, Winzeler, 1982, on the Iban.
3. Khor (2002) gave the Malaysia rate; R. Jegasothy (personal communication) provided the other figures. Likewise for the "sudden death" sub-set (20.6 per cent of all maternal mortality), the indigenous groups in West and East Malaysia had the highest rate, that is, 268 per 100,000 deliveries (Jegasothy 2002).
4. A Bidayuh woman at Mentu Tapuh told Geddes (1954*b*, p. 46) about her children, "I have seven but six I cannot see."
5. *Yearbook of Statistics*, 2003.
6. These Iban data are from Strickland and Duffield 1997; Strickland and Ulijaszek 1992, 1993, 1994.
7. In 1971, fifteen Bidayuh women surveyed by Grijpstra (1976) spent 57 per cent of their waking hours farming and 27 per cent housekeeping. With their other duties, this left them with less leisure time than the men who were surveyed. The time the women spent in farming, over 60 hours per week, necessarily included 10 or more hours spent in walking to the fields and back. Kelabit women in Bario also do most of the farm work (Hew and Sharifah 1998).
8. In addition, rural Selako women own their family's dwellings and its rice, the basis of household subsistence (Schneider 1978).
9. Many Iban women reported that when men were away, and they were left with all the farm work, they became fatigued and ill. Their children's illnesses added to their travails (Kedit 1991).
10. Geddes (1954*a*) estimated that Bidayuh farm women worked on average forty days longer per year than did men. The mitigating custom was for women to do no farm work for up to a year after childbirth.
11. Those that lived with their husband's family were pressured to return to farm work shortly after giving birth, according to Benster and Stanton (1989). Even in a resettlement area with little land made available by the government for farming, and no nearby forest for foraging, 63 per cent of the women studied were still farmers (Hew and Kedit 1987).
12. In 1996, 30 per cent of longhouse Iban women between the ages of 18 and 30 studied by Duffield and Strickland (1999) were living in urban areas as waitresses, housewives, or in other occupations. The percentage of these temporary migrants declined with age.
13. For instance, in a village 24 kilometres outside Kuching, only women attend

meetings about cleaning the village or attend PTA meetings about school issues. (Kendy Edwards, personal communication).

14. P. Lindell, personal communication.

15. <http://www.surforever.com/sam/sarawak/interviews/unidentified.html>. *The Star Online* provided more recent information on 24 September 2003 in an article by S. Then, "Longhouse Folks Affected by Bakun Project Seek Help".

16. In Sarawak, young cassava leaves are generally cooked with dried anchovies (*ikan pusu*), whereby iodine in the anchovies counteracts the goitrogenic effects of the leaves. Although cassava leaves are rich in vitamins and protein, they can contain up to 20 times the cyanide content of the tuber (Cheok 1978).

17. Recently, 7.5 per cent of Sarawak neonates were found to be iodine-deficient as a result of their mother's low iodine intake (Kiyu et al. 1998). This is significant because iodine deficiency in early life, even a mild deficit, can do life-long damage to the brain, depressing mental acuity.

18. In Bario, since 61 per cent of 229 children had intestinal parasites (Nor Aza Ahmad et al. 1998), women there may also have high infection rates.

19. *Sunday Star*, 2 July 2000, p. 12. The percentage of these cases in females was not stated.

20. *The Malaysian Today*, 27 June 2001, p. 5.

21. Grijpstra (1976) reported that 22 per cent of the Bidayuh household heads interviewed said "some women" in their village were prostitutes (p. 178), but they "are by no means treated as outcasts" (p. 110). Also, W. Koster interviewed 16 women sex workers who visited a STD clinic in Sibu in 1986 (see Appendix B in Sutlive 1991).

22. However, for both Iban (Padoch 1982) and Berawan (Metcalf 1974), pre-marital pregnancies could lead to induced abortions, to avoid social censure or shame. In both cases, a high rate of sterility was thought to ensue.

23. *Borneo Post*, 27 July 2001, p. 10. Both Thailand and Cambodia have mounted successful "100 per cent condom" campaigns; Malaysia could learn something important from these prevention efforts (Cohen 2003).

24. Sutlive (1991) noted the expectation that Iban husbands would philander when working far from home, it being one reason they took to travelling. Grijpstra (1976) noted that when married men are away from home, they often behave like bachelors. Catterall (1981) reported that doctors seldom ask men treated for STDs about their sexual contacts; this is a disservice to women who may thus have become infected. However, Linklater (1990) held that both Iban husbands and wives were sometimes promiscuous whenever they were not living together. Conversely, Kedit (1991) held that Iban moral values of marital fidelity and clean living kept most men away from brothels when they worked in the towns.

25. Bario men shun condoms (J. M. Lensy, personal communication). Iban

women have said that condoms are "unfavorable" and "funny" (Edwards 1999, 2000). Yet some Iban sex workers in Sibu say they ask men to use condoms, but they often refuse (Sutlive 1991). Men's complaints about condoms are rebutted on p. 193 in Burns et al., 1997.

26. However, some young Bidayuh women work in brothels and traveling prostitutes visit Bidayuh areas near Bau on weekends (Kiyu 1993). In like vein, promiscuity in men is not unknown. One can only wonder about the village man once considered to be the local champion in adultery (Grijpstra 1976).

27. Even though some do speak the local language, their professional speech is necessarily biased toward externally-defined problems, technologies, and logic — the mindset of modern medicine. While medicine sees health as a natural condition and illness as unnatural, some Borneo societies see illness as part of nature. For them, health is the result of living in a social group, usually a longhouse. Being away from home, being alone, saps health and causes illness (Crain 1991).

28. A Bidayuh mother in Riam went against the advice of European visitors. Her son's knife had slipped as he cut bamboo, deeply gashing his shoulder. The gash had been smeared with a mix of chilli, betel-juice spittle, "and what looked like coffee grounds" (Calder 1954, p. 30). The headman agreed the visitors should take the boy to Kuching Hospital, but the visitors soon discovered the mother and son had disappeared. The headman explained that the boy wanted to go to Kuching but his mother was afraid of hospitals and of him not being remembered: "...to be remembered one must have one's family around the death bed. To die alone is to be forgotten. To avoid that risk, the mother had smuggled him away..." (Calder 1954, p. 38).

29. Curiously, the only question they were asked about "tradition" was about the number of women in the village who wore brass anklets!

30. The Home Economics Extension Service was active in "imparting knowledge" about child care, meal planning, etc., to Bidayuh women in the Padawan area in 1990, according to Burgers and co-workers (1991).

31. In the Batang Ai resettlement area near Lubok Antu in the 1980s, 80 per cent of the women interviewed had never been to school (Hew and Kedit 1987). Bidayuh adults in the Serian area averaged only 2.2 years of schooling in 1990 (Burgers et al. 1991). Even in 1998, over 40 per cent of the young Bidayuh parents of pre-school children in Mujat village had had no formal education (Yap 1998–99).

References

MJM — Medical Journal of Malaysia
SEAJTMPH — Southeast Asian Journal of Tropical Medicine and Public Health

SMJ — *Sarawak Museum Journal*

Alexander, J., and P. Alexander. "Economic Change and Public Health in a Remote Sarawak Community". *SOJOURN* 8, no. 2 (1993): 250–74.

Anderson, A. Sarawak Pilot Applied Nutrition Project Baseline Studies Report. Department of Medical Services, Department of Agriculture, State Planning Unit, Chief Minister's Office, Kuching, 1975.

———. "Sago and Nutrition in Sarawak". *SMJ* 25 (1977): 71–80.

Ayob, A. M., et al. "A Socio-economic Study of Three SALCRA Land Schemes: Participants' Perceptions, Attitudes and Levels of Living". Faculty of Economics and Management, Universiti Putra Malaysia, Serdang, 1990.

Benster, R., and J. Stanton. "Primary Health Care for the Children of Sarawak". *Brit. J. Hosp. Med.* 42, no. 6 (1989): 488–90.

Bernama (Malaysian National News Agency). "Males Account for about 80 per cent of HIV Infections in Sarawak". 9 June 2003.

———. "Sarawak Housewives Face Increasing Risk of HIV Infection". 29 July 2004.

Burgers, P., et al. "Shifting Cultivation in Teng-Bukap Subdistrict, Kuching Division, Sarawak: A Socioeconomic Study in 16 Communities". Geographical Institute, University of Utrecht, 1991.

Burns, A. A., et al. *Where Women Have No Doctor.* Berkeley, CA: Hesperian Foundation, 1997.

Calder, R. *Men Against the Jungle.* London: Allen & Unwin, 1954.

Catterall, R. D. "Sexually Transmitted Diseases in Sabah and Sarawak". *Brit. J. Venereal Diseases* 57, no. 6 (1981): 363–66.

Chandler, G. "Access to Health Care in the interior of Sabah". In *The Political Economy of Primary Health Care in Southeast Asia*, edited by P. Cohen and J. Purcal. Canberra: Australian Development Studies Network, pp. 101–23, 1989.

Chen, P. C. Y., and P. E. P. Lim. "The Prevalence of Endemic Goitre in the Tinjar Area, Sarawak". *MJM* 37 (1982): 265–69.

Cheok, S. S. "Acute Cassava Poisoning in Children in Sarawak". *Trop. Doctor* 8, no. 3 (1978): 99–101.

Chew, D. "Social and Cultural Trends in Sarawak". *SMJ* 47 (1994): 85–100.

Chin, S. C. "Agriculture and Resource Utilization in a Lowland Rainforest Kenyah Community". *SMJ* 35 (1985): 1–322.

Christensen, H. "Fallows and Secondary Forests — A Primary Resource for Food". © Borneo Research Council, Kota Kinabalu, 2002.

Chong, G. "HIV/AIDS in Sarawak". *Sarawak Gazette* 126, no. 1539 (1999): 12–15.

Cohen, J. "HIV Gains Foothold in Key Asian Groups". *Science* 294 (2001): 282–83.

Colchester, M. *Pirates, Squatters, and Poachers.* London: Survival International, 1989.

Crain, J. B. "The Anger within the Flesh of the House: Mengalong Lun Cosmology as Argument about Babies and Birds". In *Male and Female in Borneo*, edited by V. Sutlive. Williamsburg, VA: Borneo Research Council, 1991, pp. 335–44.

De Zulueta, J. "Observations on Filariasis in Sarawak and Brunei". *Bulletin WHO* 16, no. 3 (1957): 699–705.

Duffield, A., and S. S. Strickland. Nutrition in Sarawak: Its Relationship to Development. In *Rural Development and Social Science Research. Case Studies from Borneo*, edited by V. King. Phillips, Maine: Borneo Research Council, 1999, pp. 131–58.

Edwards, J. "Cultural Perceptions of Reproduction and Family Planning Behavior among the Iban of Sarawak". Preliminary Research Report, August 1999.

———. Reproductive Beliefs and Family Planning Behavior in an Iban Community in Sarawak, Malaysia". M.S. thesis, Univ. Alabama, 2000.

Foo, L. C., et al. "Endemic Goitre in the Lemanak and Ai River Villages of Sarawak". *SEAJTMPH* 25, no. 3 (1994): 575–78.

———. "Iodization of Village Water Supply in the Control of Endemic Iodine Deficiency in Rural Sarawak, Malaysia". *Biomedical Environmental Science* 9, nos. 2–3 (1996): 236–41.

Geddes, W. R. Land Tenure of Land Dayaks. *SMJ* 6, no. 4 (1954*a*): 42–51.

———. "The Land Dayak of Sarawak". A report on the social economic survey of the Land Dayaks of Sarawak to the Colonial Social Sciences Research Council. Colonial Research Studies, no. 14. London: Her Majesty's Stationery Office, 1954*b*.

Gerrits, R. "Sustainable Development of a Village Land Use System in Upland Sarawak, East Malaysia". Ph.D. thesis, University of Queensland, 1994.

Grijpstra, B. G. *Common Efforts in the Development of Rural Sarawak, Malaysia*. Amsterdam: Van Grocum, Assen, 1976.

Hatta Solhee and J. Langub. "Challenges in Extending Development to the Penan Community in Sarawak". In *Restoration of Tropical Forest Ecosystems*, edited by H. Leith and M. Lohmann. Dordrecht: Kluwer, 1993, pp. 239–50.

Hew, C. S., and F. Kedit. "The Batang Ai Dam, Resettlement, and Rural Iban Women". In *Women Farmers and Rural Change in Asia, Toward Equal Access and Participation*, edited by N. Heyzer. Kuala Lumpur: Asia and Pacific Dev. Ctr., 1987, pp. 163–209.

Hew, C. S., and Sharifah Mariam Al-Idris. "Gender Aspects of Labour Allocation and Decision-making in Agricultural Production: A Case Study of the Kelabits in Bario Highlands, Sarawak". In *Bario, the Kelabit Highlands of Sarawak*, edited by Ghazally Ismail and Laily bin Din. Petaling Jaya: Pelanduk, 1998, pp. 307–30.

Huang, M. "HIV/AIDS among Fishers: Vulnerability to their Partners". In *Global Symposium on Women in Fisheries*, edited by M. J. Williams et al. Penang, Malaysia: ICLARM, 2002, pp. 49–53.

Ireson, C. J. *Field, Forest, and Family: Women's Work and Power in Laos.* Boulder, CO: Westview Press, 1996.

Ireson-Doolittle, C., and G. Moreno-Black. *The Lao.* Boulder, CO: Westview Press, 2003.

Ismail, M. N., et al. "Obesity in Malaysia". *Obesity Reviews* 3: 203–208, 2002.

Jegasothy, R. "Sudden Maternal Deaths in Malaysia: A Case Report". *J. Obstet. Gynaecol. Res.* 28, no. 4 (2002): 186–93.

Jha, P., et al. "Reducing HIV Transmission in Developing Countries". *Science* 292 (2001): 224–25.

Kamil, M. A., and C. L. Teng. "Rural Health Care in Malaysia". *Aust. J. Rural Health* 10 (2002): 99–103.

Kedit, P. M. " 'Meanwhile Back Home…': Bejalai and their Effects on Iban Men and Women". In *Female and Male in Borneo*, edited by V. Sutlive. Williamsburg, VA: Borneo Research Council, 1991, pp. 295–316.

Khor, G. L. "Micronutrient Deficiency and its Alleviation: The Case of Malaysia". *Asia Pac. J. Clin. Nutr., Suppl.* 1, 11, no. 3 (2002): S377.

Kiyu, A. "Epidemiology of Cancer in Sarawak". *SEAJTMPH* 16, no. 4 (1985): 584–90.

———. Comments. In Bidayuh Cultural Seminar, vol. 2, session IV, paper no. 9, pp. 2–3. Kuching, 1993.

Kiyu, A., et al. "Iodine Deficiency Disorders in Sarawak, Malaysia". *Asia Pacific J. Clin. Nutr.* 7: 256–61, 1998.

Leete, R., and K. Kwok. "Demographic Changes in East Malaysia and their Relationship with those of the Peninsula 1960–1980". *Pop. Studies* 40 (1986): 83–100.

Linklater, A. *Wild People.* New York: Atlantic Monthly Press, 1900.

Lye, M. S., et al. "Patterns of Risk Behavior for Patients with Sexually Transmitted Diseases and Surveillance for Human Immunodeficiency Virus in Kuala Lumpur, Malaysia". *Internat. J. STD & AIDS* 5 (1994): 124–29.

Maberly, G., and C. Eastman. "Endemic Goitre in Sarawak". *SEAJTMPH* 7, no. 3 (1976): 434–42.

Metcalf, P. Berawan adoption practices. *SMJ* 22 (1974): 275–86.

Nagaraj, S., and S. R. Yahya. "Prostitution in Malaysia". In *The Sex Sector*, edited by L. L. Lin. Geneva: International Labour Office, 1998, pp. 67–99.

Nor Aza Ahmad et al. "Distribution of Intestinal Parasites in a Community of Kelabit School Children". In *Bario, the Kelabit Highlands of Sarawak*, edited by Ghazally Ismail and Laily bin Din. Petaling Jaya: Pelanduk, 1998, pp. 261–66.

Noeb, L. M. "Some Aspects of the Social Customs of the Bidayuh of Sarawak". *SMJ* 47 (1994): 127–35.

Ogihara, T., et al. Endemic Goitre in Sarawak, Borneo Island: Prevalence and Pathogenesis. *Endocrin. Japan* 19, no. 3 (1972a): 285–93.

———. Serum Thyrotropic Levels of Natives in Sarawak. *J. Clin. Endocrin. Metab.* 35, no. 5 (1972*b*): 711–15.

Oldrey, T. Medical report. *SMJ* 20 (1972): 270–77.

Padoch, C. "Migration and its Alternatives among the Iban of Sarawak". The Hague: Martinus Nijhoff, 1982.

Pelletier, D. "The Role of Qualitative Methodologies in Nutritional Surveillance". In *Rapid Assessment Procedures*, edited by *N. Scrimshaw and G. Gleason.* Boston, MA: INFDC, 1992, pp. 51–59.

Polunin, I. "Endemic Goitre in Malaysia". Assignment Report, Malaysia 5607-E(0081). Regional Office for the Western Pacific, World Health Organization, 1971.

Rabi'ah Abdul Ghani and A. Kiyu. "Knowledge and Attitudes of AIDS Seminar Participants Regarding Various Aspects of HIV Infection". *Sarawak Gazette* 122 no. 1533 (1995): 20–24.

Rashidah Abdullah. "Towards Women's Health Needs". In *Asia-Pacific Post-Beijing Implementation Monitor: Health*, edited by V. Griffith. Kuala Lumpur: Asia and Pacific Dev. Ctr., 1999, pp. 341–45.

Rintos Mail. "Sarawak has Highest Reported STD Cases". *The Malaysian Today*, 27 June 2001, p. 5.

Rokiah Ismail. "HIV/AIDS in Malaysia". *AIDS* 12 (suppl. B): S33-S41, 1998.

Sagin, D. D., et al. "Intestinal Parasitic Infection among Five Interior Communities at Upper Rejang River, Sarawak, Malaysia". *SEAJTMPH* 33, no. 1 (2002*a*): 18–22.

———. "Anemia in Remote Interior Communities in Sarawak, Malaysia". *SEAJTMPH* 33, no. 2 (2002*b*): 373–77.

Sarawak Government. <http://Sarawak.health.gov.my/stats/hfacts97/>, 1997.

Schneider, W. "The Bilik Family of the Selako Dayak of Western Borneo". In *Sarawak — Linguistics and Development Problems*. Studies in Third World Societies, vol. 3. Williamsburg, VA, 1978, pp. 139–65.

Sellato, B. "Salt in Borneo". *Le sel de la vie en Asie du Sud-est*, edited by P. La Roux and J. Ivanoff. Prince of Songkla University, Thailand, 1993, pp. 263–84.

Strickland, S. S., and A. Duffield. "Anthropometric Status and Resting Metabolic Rate in Users of the Areca Nut and Smokers of Tobacco in Rural Sarawak". *Annals Hum. Biol.* 25, no. 3 (1997): 453–74.

Strickland, S. S., and S. Ulijaszek. "Energy Nutrition of Iban of Song and Kanowit, February–April 1990". *SMJ* 43 (1992): 135–96.

———. "Resting Energy Expenditure and Body Composition in Rural Sarawak Adults". *Amer. J. Hum. Biol.* 5 (1993): 341–50.

———. "Body Mass Index and Illness in Rural Sarawak". *Europ. J. Clin. Nutr.* 48, Suppl. 3: S98-S109, 1994.

Sushama, P. C. "Health and Welfare Services for Elderly People in Malaysia". In

Ageing in East and Southeast Asia, edited by D. Phillips. London: Edward Arnold, 1992, pp. 167–84.

Sutlive, V. Keling and Kumang. "Town: Differential Effects of Urban Migration on Iban Men and Women". In *Female and Male in Borneo*, edited by V. Sutlive. Williamsburg, VA: Borneo Research Council, 1991, pp. 489–528.

Tee, E. S., et al. "School-administered Weekly Iron-folate Supplements Improve Hemoglobin and Ferritin Concentrations in Malaysian Adolescent Girls". *Amer. J. Clin. Nutr.* 69 (1999): 1249–56.

Wai, B. H. K., S. Singh, and S. L. Varma. "HIV Infection in Females Dependent on Drugs". *Addiction* 91, no. 3 (1996): 435–38.

Windle, J., and R. Cramb. "Roads, Remoteness, and Rural Development: Social Impacts of Rural Roads in Upland Areas of Sarawak, Malaysia". In *Rural Development and Social Science Research: Case Studies from Borneo*, edited by V. King. Phillips, ME: Borneo Research Council, 1999, pp. 215–50.

Winzeler, R. "Sexual Status in Southeast Asia: Comparative Perspectives on Women, Agriculture, and Political Organization". In *Women in Southeast Asia*, edited by P. Van Esterick. Center for Southeast Asian Studies. Northern Illinois University, 1982, pp. 176–213.

Wong, L. M. "Government Dental Services in Sarawak, East Malaysia". Dental Update 19, no. 10 (1992): 430–32.

WWF (Malaysia). "Proposals for a Conservation Strategy for Sarawak". Report prepared for the Government of Sarawak by the World Wildlife Fund (Malaysia), Kuala Lumpur, 1985.

Yaakub, N. F., A, M. Ayob, and T. Noweg. "Dayak Bidayuh of the Bau-Lundu Region: Demographic Profile and their Perception of Educational Amenities". *SMJ* 44 (1993): 77–91.

Yadav, A. "Low Birth Weight Incidence in Lundu, Sarawak". *MJM* 49, no. 2 (1994): 164–68.

Yap, C. P. "Nutritional Assessment of Bidayuh Children Aged between Two to Six years old in Serian District, Sarawak". B. Sci. thesis, Faculty of Medicine and Health Science, Universiti Putra Malaysia, Serdang, 1998–99.

Yearbook of Statistics, Sarawak. Sarawak Government, Kuching, 2003.

4

Madness and the Hegemony of Healing
The Legacy of Colonial Psychiatry in Sarawak

Sara Ashencaen Crabtree

Introduction

This chapter considers how the adoption of psychiatric values and practices imported from Europe in the nineteenth century has had an impact on local populations in the Malayan region, with a specific focus on Sarawak. In doing so, it draws upon two main areas of discussion. The first focuses on how psychiatry as a discipline has traditionally sought scientific and cultural hegemony in relation to existing and adapting healing methods that are indigenous to this region. Psychiatric service user views are used in conjunction with those of traditional healers to illustrate the issues that emerge from this background of competing and overlapping paradigms of healing. The second part considers two aspects of the process of socialization that women patients experience upon hospitalization in terms of gendered notions of appropriate care that is not always closely compatible with traditional and cultural norms.

This account is supported primarily by findings developed from a recently completed ethnographic study of mental health and women service users in Sarawak. The study sought to privilege the experiences of patients at a local psychiatric hospital and serves to balance more numerous, medically orientated studies focusing only on the pathology of psychiatric service users (Arif and Maniam 1995; Osman and Ainsah 1994; Ramli 1989; Varma and Sharma 1995). Narratives from both female and male patients were originally solicited in relation to personal experiences of contemporary psychiatric institutional care and personal meanings attached to these accounts. These were balanced by views from staff and other caregivers and these served to contextualize polarized ideologies of care. Finally, these accounts are set against the historical backdrop of psychiatric care in Borneo and Malaya that has been informed and shaped by medical practices that can be traced back to prevalent practices and attitudes imported during the colonial period.

Sarawak Women in Psychiatric Care: Research Narratives

Although many of the experiences of patients were equally shared by both men and women, especially with regard to medical treatment, in other areas findings indicated sharply defined gender differentials. Here the condition of women patients as understood and described by themselves, was both illuminating and powerful in the implied or overt critique of social norms and social forces, where the resulting pressures of society bear down oppressively on women who cannot or are unable to conform to convention. The powerful institutions of psychiatry and the judiciary can often be seen to work in collusion in the lives of non-conformists and social misfits, thus relegating their voices to the narrowest margins of credibility and the audible. The voices of perceived women deviants are likely to be the most silenced of all.

Thus the narratives of women psychiatric patients here are used to graphically illustrate the issues of gender and ethnicity in relation to a diagnosis of mental illness. This author's understanding of how the women interviewed perceived their symbolic and literal fall from social acceptance was further illuminated by feminist critiques. From this research experience a *praxis* developed: a cross-fertilization between theory and research findings. This permitted flesh to be put on the otherwise rather bare feminist theoretical skeleton of what it would be like to be a woman under those material and specific social conditions, as well as how unique or universally applicable these experiences were for Sarawak women in psychiatric care.

Colonialism and Psychiatry in Borneo and Malaya

The history of medical developments in Borneo together with Malaya in general is a complex one. One might presuppose that there was little in the way of effective care prior to its migration from Europe and adoption in the region, primarily from the early nineteenth century onwards. Yet this is to ignore or trivialize how important traditional healing methods were to their respective communities and the way these have been adapted over time up to the present day (Gullick 1987; Humholtz 1991).

In the nineteenth century, health care in this region was concentrated in the urban areas of colonial authority and relegated to the needs of primarily European expatriates, mainly in the militia and navy (Baba 1992; Bhugra 2001; Deva 1992; Manderson 1996). It was only later that the needs of others were catered for and these too would predominantly be migrants, but in this case from Asia. Thus, the sites of earliest established asylums were in Malaya. In Penang in 1829, for example, a site of the earliest established asylums, Chinese and Indian males formed the greatest majority of patients, eclipsing a much smaller number of female counterparts and the indigenous population (Jin Inn Teoh 1971, p. 22).

This picture would be repeated at the Singapore asylums and others in Malaya, as well as later in Sarawak. Whereas the local population tended at first to adhere to their own healing traditions and were unlikely to seek alien medical practices unless pressed by necessity, voluntarily or otherwise. Nonetheless once commenced, establishing Western medical practices, in which one can include psychiatry, was an inexorable process that would culminate in becoming the dominant paradigm of healing.

In rural societies like Sarawak and Malaya, traditional healing practices were often associated by Europeans as being a primitive, backwater enterprise compared with the modern, urban-based care offered by imperialism. Consequently the policy of siting psychiatric asylums in conurbations stood in some contrast to those of nineteenth-century Britain where the "ideal asylum" was a huge self-sustaining establishment set in some conveniently remote location where it would cause minimum offence to the local neighbourhood (Prior 1993, p. 26). The Sarawak Mental Hospital built in 1957, unlike the early asylums in Malaya, more closely resembled those British establishments, being at the time isolated from the nearest conurbation by thick jungle. Built to cater for a local and indigenous population, its inaccessible situation demanded a veritable migration for the afflicted individual, in its remoteness, from familiar surroundings. Later in the twentieth century however, with the receding of the rain forest due to the forces of urbanization, this hospital would revert to standing as a symbol of modernization as well as that of cultural dislocation in terms of healing practices.

It would be a mistake, however, to assume that healing traditions in the general region were utterly condemned out of hand by the colonials. On the contrary the response was more likely to be indifference or even tolerance, as in the worst case these traditions were considered fairly harmless. They had the added advantage of relieving the colonial authorities of having to provide essential medical care for communities that were remote or reluctant to avail themselves of European healthcare (Manderson 1966).

European observers have long entertained an anthropological interest in regional phenomena from the eighteenth century onwards. At the turn of the twentieth century Emile Kraepelin, for example, carried out extensive travels in Java and Malaya noting regional manifestations of mental disorder (McCulloch 2001, p. 78). Likewise throughout most of his career in Sarawak, Dr K. E. Schmidt, the "Government specialist alienist" and director of the former Sarawak Mental Hospital, was busily engaged in the study of the ethnic and cultural peculiarities amongst patient populations in Sarawak (Chiu et al. 1972; Nissom and Schmidt 1967; Schmidt 1961; Schmidt 1964). Whilst maintaining a sympathetic and positive outlook of the benefits of traditional healing on local Dayak communities.

> As mental health workers in other parts of the world, it has become clear to us in Sarawak also, that native healers play an important part in the treatment especially of mental illness. They have done so successfully for centuries before modern scientific psychiatry ever came to the Sarawak scene (Schmidt 1964, p. 150).

The development of psychiatry in Borneo in the nineteenth century however, was one greatly overshadowed by the far greater need to overcome the virulent epidemics that could decimate entire communities of local people as well as migrants from Asia and Europe. Whatever mental distress existed in the Borneo region, this was likely to have been largely the repercussion of plagues and the pervasive and oppressive backdrop of political domination, debt slavery, localized warfare and trophy head-hunting; all of which tended to besiege small communities for long periods of time. The prevalence of mental illness amongst individuals is therefore uncertain and little remarked upon in the few existing accounts available. It is likely, however, to have held a low priority as a health issue compared to the physical hazards that seem to have been a yearly event in which women and children were considered to be the most vulnerable to the psychological strains of uncertainty and fear (Knapen 1979; Nieuwenhuis 1929).

Traditional Healing in Contemporary Society

Today research indicates that traditional healing practices, far from declining, have successfully survived (Ashencaen Crabtree and Chong 1999; Barrett 1993; Barrett 1997; Bentelspacher et al. 1994; Razali 1995; Razali et al. 1996; Razali 1997). Furthermore traditional healing practices and conventional biomedical care are frequently sought in tandem by psychiatric patients or in cycles, depending on the perceived needs of patients as well as their view of the effectiveness of treatment.

These practices are nonetheless held in uneasy tension with a more aggressive protagonist. Conventional medicine or "biomedicine", is no longer conceived of as solely Western, so much as ubiquitous and international. It retains its dominance through having greater social authority in its alliance with the processes of law as well as through its mandate to proscribe normality and deviance. Yet the Cartesian dualism inherent in biomedicine is not one that travels and assimilates easily with other cultures that may not accept the basic premises of biomedicine. Premises such as the separation of mind and body, that sickness is largely devoid of personal meaning; and that asking *why* rather than *how* a person has fallen ill is an irrelevant question for the physician.

Abnormal or unusual mental states in an individual are normally ascribed to mental illness by psychiatrists but are more likely to be construed by local ethnic communities in Sarawak as the possession of the soul. The task of the healer is to restore the spirit to its owner through the reaffirmation of the necessary distinctions between the spheres of the living and the dead; for incursions by the latter are responsible for disorders, disease and general chaos. Sacred ritual achieves this end by restoring order and good health. The *serará bunga*, an Iban mourning ceremony in which flowers are used to achieve this necessary distinction, is one that many psychiatric patients across cultural boundaries have received as particularly appropriate for their form of suffering (Ashencaen Crabtree and Chong 1999; Barrett 1993, p. 240).

Despite, or maybe owing to the popularity of traditional healing rituals such as this one, psychiatric practitioners tend to regard them with, at best, ambivalence. Traditional healing methods may be seen as either a harmless diversion or worse: one that may endorse and validate the individual's misconceptions of the nature of as well as the proper treatment for a serious condition. That said, it is interesting to note that traditional healers themselves claim that in particularly intransigent cases of disorder, medical staff may covertly refer patients to them whilst overtly regarding such practices as anachronistic and irrelevant in a modern healthcare system.

There is, however, a body of research that strongly indicates positive outcomes for sufferers where cultural beliefs foster the view that disorders have their source in external factors, are curable and that the individual can attain re-integration back into their community. This stands in direct contrast to the deep stigma and associated marginalization of psychiatric patients as seen particularly in the West, in which as Warner points out:

> This may explain why even those individuals who are treated in modern Western-style hospitals and clinics in the developing world rather than by indigenous therapists may experience a higher recovery rate from psychosis. (Warner 1996, p. 61)

In this way it can be understood that the traditional healer occupies an ambiguous but critical role in the interplay between psychiatric diagnosis and cultural constructs of the nature and cause of the affliction. Equally, that diagnosis and treatment that differs markedly from the sufferer's schema are likely to be less willingly accepted and probably less efficacious in general, as will be discussed further.

The Traditional Healing Trade

Diversity of alternative traditional treatment flourishes in cities, towns as well as rural locations in association with the ethnic populations that tend to cluster in these areas. Logically one would suppose a city-based Chinese traditional healer, like the well-known *dang ke* Mr Chua,[1] would be likely to service an exclusively urban Chinese local population, while *Puan* Junita, a successful Iban *manang* (shaman) who operates from her remote longhouse cabin, might rarely receive anyone from the far-off conurbations. Apparently not so, in interview both claim that they see a wide range of individuals, from all walks of life, with all kinds of complaints. Patients are from all the major ethnic communities, the only proviso being that the healer has a good reputation. Thus to transverse rugged or unfamiliar terrain is no deterrence for determined patients and families seeking a cure. As Mr Chua noted on the subject of working across cultural boundaries:

> Yes, I have treated patients from different religions, such as Christians, Buddhists, Taoists and even Malays who are Muslim ... I have some knowledge of the different religions and understand their different

teachings. This gives me an advantage (because) I can understand their beliefs. If we (avoid) emphasizing that our religion is the best, and can accept and respect the religion of others, it will be acceptable to patients.... As we know Islam greatly emphasizes religion and we should see their situation through their religion. We have to understand that when a patient is sick and seeks for your help, there is no boundary because I am a Taoist and you are a Muslim. They (patients) are sincere in seeking for your help. Even in the Koran there is a passage stating that "When you are suffering seek help from anyone who can save your life". Thus, Muslims themselves understand and if they have looked for treatment in the hospital or elsewhere and their condition didn't get better, they will seek help from you.

Puan Juanita would doubtless agree. She explains that many of her visitors have been disappointed by the care they have received at hospitals and doctors' clinics, and where they have failed, she often succeeds, particularly in cases of broken *pantang* (taboo) and spirit possession. While bogus healers exist and ply a trade amongst the credulous, says Mr Chua, such individuals will be revealed by their lack of success in due course. Both he and *Puan* Junita regard themselves instead as following a vocation and take an ecumenical stance in treating the public, seeing themselves as merely different in kind and approach from conventional medics but with the same willingness to devote themselves to the care and cure of patients regardless of ethnicity and culture.

While traditional healing is sought across urban/rural divides, community attitudes towards mental illness do not appear to markedly differ between specific ethnic groups living in either location, in terms of higher levels of tolerance towards those with mental illness. Research findings indicate that relatives across ethnic groups located in both urban and rural areas were equally concerned by behaviours such as emotional distress, disturbed sleeping habits and compulsive types of behaviour, although aimless wandering was considered to be somewhat less of a hazard in rural areas. Relatives also showed a particular concern for unorthodox behaviour by women, particularly if this related to the transgression of sexual mores (Ashencaen Crabtree 1999*a*).

Patient Perspectives of Psychiatric Treatment

In this study the issues of individual interpretation of mental illness and the patient response to treatment were not significantly marked by gender differentials. Rather this was one area in which women and men tended to agree as being unpleasant and unnatural when compared with traditional healing methods. As one young Dayak woman on her first admission comments, "It's weird that everyone here is sleepy and weak after taking medication. It may be good but it makes people so weak, and always sleeping."

In general, however, medication regimes during hospitalization were complied with, due in large part to coercive enforcement policies, and consequently resented by patients. Upon discharge patients were likely to stop taking their prescription and "medication defaulting" was seen as the major cause for "revolving-door" re-admissions (Lau and Hardin 1996). Far more feared than pills and depot injections were the ordeals of electron-convulsive therapy (ECT) that most psychiatric patients appeared to have experienced, and repeatedly, over the course of their psychiatric careers.

Jane Ussher contends that in Britain ECT has been particularly associated with the treatment of women, especially those who consciously or otherwise subverted gender norms. Significantly there is no evidence to suggest that a similar preponderance exists in psychiatric facilities in Sarawak (Ussher 1991, p. 163). Nonetheless, ECT seems common enough and here a dialogue with women patients describes the experience of ECT in highly graphic albeit lyrical terms:

Aini: When not well — when mind is chronic — your speaking not a structure — imagine things — hearing voices. ECT — with a current all over your head and a wire in your hand — a needle in your hand.... Vibrations of sound make us giddy — it radiates the mind in circulation... First an injection is given, half asleep, half aware — feeling of something afloat — drifting slowly and slowly — fast asleep. Like a thunder moving with a storm. Like a sea breeze with the wave.... Very painful and giddy [holding temples] vomiting — under our chest got pain... When I got my third ECT this year, when I was 36 (years old) — I was awake twenty-five minutes...

               [It is uncertain what Aini meant when she said she was "awake" as she also said she was under anaesthetic, that is, "asleep"].

Researcher: Can you remember afterwards?

Aini: Not yet actually ...We remember things, slowly remember.

Researcher:	Do you think ECT is a good sort of medication?
Aini:	Not very good, ECT. Sometimes destroys our organic systems.
Soo Mei:	If I am unhappy, it makes you feel more happy, but cannot help you.
Aini:	Sometimes you remember — sometimes you forget — like waves.
Maria:	Bad memory. ECT no good, bad memory. Six times! [Received ECT]. Pills better.
Tuyah:	Whole body shaking — electricalized.

In conclusion, non-compliance towards treatment is habitually interpreted by staff as due to a lack of insight. It is therefore seen as a symptom of sickness, rather than a fairly obvious form of protest and resistance. Interpretations that pathologize the individual effectively neutralize political actions of resistance whilst continuing to confirm that the individual is both sick and irresponsible. In addition the message of psychiatry is that mental illness is not so much curable as treatable. That in effect diagnosed individuals, like cancer patients, may hope for a remission but can never describe themselves as completely cured of mental illness. By comparison traditional healing is overtly optimistic, its message and methods work towards the complete restoration of the individual (and for some ethnic groups the tainted family as well). While for psychiatry if biomedicine continues to struggle for hegemony amongst plural forms of traditional treatment, the ultimately victory is by no means assured in Sarawak at least.

Women's Madness — The Process of Socialization

If medication and treatment appeared to stand as gender-neutral activities imposed on patients, this was not representative of general hospital practices that in fact tended to draw marked distinctions in the care of men and women. This stands in general accord with traditional psychiatric practice that has traditionally focused on women as particularly susceptible to mental illness and therefore liable to particular forms of supervision.

In the nineteenth century large numbers of women were admitted to psychiatric care in English psychiatric institutions. Insanity as a gendered condition predates even this period, and from the seventeenth century onwards the medical profession was particularly interested in "specifically female problems" (Russell 1995, p. 18; Showalter 1983, p. 3). Feminine pathology, typified by melancholia and hysteria, was dominated by the medical preoccupation with female sexuality and moral purity which were seen as the underlying causation of these disorders (Kromm 1994).

The twentieth century has seen a huge predominance of women diagnosed with mental illness globally (Miles 1988, p. 2; Ramon 1996, p. 85; Ussher 1991, p. 163). Phyllis Chesler states that more women are being hospitalized with a diagnosis of mental illness than "at any other time in history" (1996, p. 46). Wetzel (2000) argues that in both the developed and developing world, global conditions of oppression affect women living in patriarchal societies, such as Malaysia. These forms of oppression towards women include low status, poverty and exploitation, sexual violence and other acts of human rights violation (Barnes and Bowl 2001, p. 74).

As a dominant and pervading force, patriarchy has always been preoccupied with the issues of women's sexuality and fertility and the need to control them. The male-dominated emerging profession of psychiatry as a global influence and institution remains preoccupied with notions of feminine moral purity and its antithesis. This continues as a dominant discourse in the relation to the labelling of women as suffering from mental illness. Research findings suggest that this appears to be as true of Malaysian women psychiatric patients today as their Western counterparts, while the free movement of women has often been viewed as a dangerous liberty and an incitement to immorality (Barnes and Bowl 2001, p. 72; Ussher 1991, p. 71).

Hospitalized women psychiatric patients in Sarawak were found to be subject to far more draconian measures with regard to their free access to the wider hospital. While the movements of male patients were severely curtailed during their periods in locked wards, being liberated onto the open ward often gave them the added privilege of leaving the ward altogether (although not the hospital grounds) for periods of time. Most women by contrast were not permitted this liberty except for certain post-menopausal women whose age and assumed asexuality were regarded as sufficiently protective in themselves. Yet, to put matters into context, if the free movement of women inside the hospital setting is compromised so severely, this may represent merely a further and more radical stage in the control of women's freedom most particularly seen in the rural setting.

In Sarawak, among certain ethnic groups, the right to access the world beyond the boundaries of the immediate rural community is one that belongs primarily to men. For the Iban, prestige is achieved through *bejalai*, in which men may leave the longhouse community for months and years on end in the quest for adventure, material acquisition and employment typically found in urban conurbations. However, this is an exclusively male activity while the role of women is to ensure through their labour the survival of the community back home. A woman who seeks to emulate the freedom of men in this regard is seen as highly disreputable and may reap the consequences of this notoriety as a result (Kedit 1991, p. 297; Sutlive 1991, p. 494).

While many male patients participating in this study were unmarried individuals who moved sporadically between the parental home and institutional care, many of the women interviewed were married mothers. The enforced separation of mothers from their children by the powers of custodial care and collusion by husbands and extended family was not an uncommon hazard for women. Elynna, a Dayak woman from a rural community, typified how women were more likely than male counterparts to lose not only their social standing and their freedom but also their children, if tainted with immorality.

Elynna's was a tragic and typical tale of gender oppression and loss, in which her marriage failed when her husband left to set up home with another woman and then refused to support his former family. Becoming increasingly impoverished in her rural community, she migrated to the city with her children in order to find work and while life continued to be hard for her, the family survived. One day her husband suddenly appeared and took the children from her, depositing them with one of her distant relatives, on the grounds that Elynna was earning a living as a prostitute, an accusation she absolutely denied. A year passed without her being allowed to see the children and to add to her injuries, she was cast off by the rest of her family. The terrible anxieties she was under resulted in a sudden state of disorientation, which she describes as "unconsciousness" in public, which resulted in her being forcibly escorted by the police to the hospital where she remained under custody. Now under medication she had regained her senses but continued to be beset with worry and frustration, especially as she had been informed that there were moves afoot to formally adopt the children within the family against her wishes.

Elynna powerfully conveyed her belief that it was the accusation of immorality that had unlawfully, but not uniquely, deprived her of her children, driving her temporarily and understandably out of her mind. She had little doubt that her decision to move to the city was viewed as suspect by the family, and her endeavour to find some kind of employment amongst strangers tantamount to a loss of respectability. Far from applauding her initiative in seeking a new life for herself and her children, this action had tainted her, perhaps irrevocably so. Her hospitalization acted as the final proof that she was unfit to be a mother, wife and accepted member of her rural community.

Lessons from Capitalism — the Unequal Labour of Men and Women

Gender norms also serve to demarcate the labour of men and women in psychiatric care. Long-stay hospital patients are normally expected to while away the hours undertaking various forms of work. Patient labour is typically deployed in three main areas, firstly to undertake tasks that enable the institution to run effectively. These may involve a variety of basic cleaning tasks on the ward such as washing up plates, irrespective of the use of professional agency cleaners. Secondly, patients are used to supervise and assist others who are less competent mentally as well as physically, and these latter duties are considered particularly appropriate for women. Thirdly, patients are allocated occupational therapy tasks that are once again divided along a hierarchical scale of skills with, in this instance, remuneration commensurate with sexist practices. These contrasts with the notions of the much-lauded complementary nature of rural work for ethnic communities in Sarawak in particular and Southeast Asia in general (Atkinson 1990; Mashman 1991; Rousseau 1991; Schneider and Schneider 1991).

Occupational therapy work for men involves carpentry, basket weaving and small-scale livestock farming. Incentives are given in the form of financial reimbursement, in which farming is seen as the most lucrative, albeit remaining a paltry figure by commercial standards. At least, for men in this kind of work there is the potential for the development of skills as well as the utilization of existing ones. Women by contrast are allocated work of the most monotonous and de-skilling variety — that of thread-sorting, where rags are picked clean of their threads and used as stuffing material for upholstery and soft toys that others, not they, will make. Predictably this kind of handicraft pays by far the least in a system already underpinned by obvious exploitation.

Moreover, while psychiatric patients are often viewed in the public's mind as an unproductive drain on society, the hospital system has universally always relied on the largely unpaid labour of patients like these for its continued existence (Black 1988; Barham 1992). The experience of women service users in this study however, indicates that further measures were experimented with in the attempt to extract further labour from them as well as to mould them into future compliant workers.

Ah Ming, for example, was a multiple admitted Chinese woman who had been unusually given a factory-type punch-card by Dr B, one of the few psychiatrists at the hospital, ensuring that a certain number of hours were devoted to her work. Her role at home was that of an impoverished, aging spinster sister reliant on the unwilling charity of the family. As the "poor relative" she acted as an unpaid if somewhat unreliable domestic servant, but more than this her diagnosis marked her out for exclusion as a pariah. An angry woman, her resentment occasionally resulted in violent quarrels with family members in which Ah Ming tended to come off the worst, followed by a prompt re-admission to hospital. The rigorous training Ah Ming was subjected to through the punch-card system seemed designed to discipline her into uncomplaining, ill-paid, unfulfilling and mind-numbing tedious work compatible with her stigmatized station in life as a woman with a psychiatric history. When this was accomplished to the satisfaction of staff, she would be considered fit for discharge back to the dubious care of her family.

Assembly-line production work, typical of industrialized societies, is accordingly often considered particularly suitable for women and not merely those institutionalized by the psychiatric hospital system. Aihwa Ong (1990) describes the process in which Malay *kampung* girls have been seen as a useful industrial commodity to be duly pressed into bench-assembly work for Japanese electronics companies. The following description of the factory floor could just as easily be used to describe the work of women patients in the hospital setting. "Thus nimble fingers, fine eyesight, and, by implication, the passivity to withstand low skill, unstimulating work are said to be biological attributes unique to women" (Ong 1990, p. 396).

If, as Hew Cheng Sim notes, agricultural work is demanding in rural communities, the tempo of work is at least controlled by the women themselves, who manage to combine the labours of childcare with those of the land far more harmoniously than can be achieved in an urban factory (Hew 2003, p. 97). While in turn Ong regards work back in the *kampung* as being not only more autonomous, but more varied and demanding of multiple skills (Ong 1990, p. 405).

In the hospital setting however, it is somewhat doubtful whether handicraft work as undertaken by women patients could be viewed as authentically gender normative within the cultural context of Sarawak in which skilled domestic work has always been conducted along with farming and mercantile activities (Yee 2001, p. 3). Instead this work, oppressive in its tedium and futility, appeared to conform more closely with sexist stereotypes mirroring the economic inequalities inherent in conventional patriarchal, capitalistic and urbanized societies, where the labour of girls and women are the least rewarded of all (Wetzel 2000; Witz 1992).

Conclusion

The common thread that links the history of psychiatric care in Malaysia to the accounts of Malaysian women psychiatric patients in Sarawak is that of migration of cultural healing forms. In the case of psychiatry, it has made a successful transition in moving from the urban centres of nineteenth century colonial control to a ubiquitous position across rural and urban settings in twentieth century Malaysia. However, while it has played an indisputably important medical role in many respects, it has also carried many historical assumptions and prejudices towards women and ethnic groups that have become unwelcome characteristics in many of its encounters with these groups.

Critiques of psychiatry have pointed out the cultural dissonance of its premises, not to mention methods, in treating non-Western people. Traditional healing methods in Malaysia at least, have adapted to the aggressive claims of psychiatry and biomedicine in general, and continue to maintain a firm foothold in healing local populations. Any discomfort felt with tandem care by conventional medics and traditional healers appears to lie with the former rather than the latter or the local people they mutually care for.

For women, psychiatry's continued preoccupation with issues of morality and sexuality have merely added to the universal oppression by patriarchy, in all its diverse forms. As the research narratives convey, a fateful synergy has been created by reframing morality in terms of pathology standing in combination with ethnocentric views of femininity and conventional mores. Local women may themselves be struggling with sexist strategies in their own communities that serve to disempower them in seeking an independent life in contemporary urbanized society. It is therefore all the more tragic that these struggles can then be viewed as pathology, a judgement endorsed at both community level and through the arbitration of psychiatry.

Note

1. The names of research participants have been changed in the interest of confidentiality.

References

Arif, N. H. and T. Maniam. "Chronic Schizophrenia and Family Burden in an Urban Sample". *Malaysian Journal of Psychiatry* 3, no. 2 (1995): 59–63.

Ashencaen Crabtree, S. "Stigma and Exclusion: Implications for Community Psychiatric Services in Sarawak, Malaysia". *Asia Pacific Journal of Social WorkInternational Journal* 9, no. 1 (1999a): 114–26.

Ashencaen Crabtree, S. and G. Chong. "Psychiatric Outreach Work in Sarawak, Malaysia". *Breakthrough International Journal* 2, no. 4 (1999): 49–60.

Atkinson, J. M. "How Gender Makes a Difference in Wana Society". In *Power and Difference: Gender in Island Southeast Asia*, edited by Jane Monnig Atkinson and Shelly Errington. Stanford, California: Stanford University Press, 1990.

Baba, I. "Social Work — An Effort towards Building a Caring Society". In *Caring Society: Emerging Issues and Future Directions*, edited by C. K. Sin and I. M. Salleh. Malaysia: Institute of Strategic and International Studies.

Barnes, M. and R. Bowl. *Taking over the Asylum*. Basingstoke: Palgrave, 2001.

Barrett, R. J. "Performance, Effectiveness and the Iban Manang". In *The Seen and the Unseen: Shamanism, Mediumship and Possession in Borneo*, edited by R. L. Winzeler. Virginia, USA: Ashley Printing Services, 1993.

Barrett, J. "Cultural Formulation of Psychiatric Diagnosis: *Sakit Gila* in an Iban Longhouse: Chronic Schizophrenia". *Culture, Medicine and Psychiatry* 21 (1997): 365–79.

Bentelspacher, C. E., et al. "Coping and Adaptation Patterns among Chinese, Indian and Malay Families Caring for a Mentally Ill Relative". *Families in Society: The Journal of Contemporary Human Services* (May 1994): 287–94.

Bhugra, D. "The Colonized Psyche: British Influence on Indian Psychiatry" . In *Colonialism and Psychiatry*, edited by D. Bhugra and R. Littlewood. Oxford: Oxford University Press, 2001.

Chesler, P. "Women and Madness: The Mental Asylum". In *Speaking Our Minds: An Anthology of Personal Experiences of Mental Distress and Its*

Consequences, edited by J. Read and J. Reynolds. Houndsmill, Basingstoke: The Open University/Macmillan Press Ltd, 1996.

Chiu, T. L., et al. "A Clinical and Survey Study of Ltah in Sarawak, Malaysia". *Psychological Medicine* 2 (1972): 155–65.

Deva, M. P. "Psychiatry and Mental Health in Malaysia: Current State and Future Directions". In *Caring Society: Emerging Issues and Future Directions*, edited by C. K. Sin and I. M. Salleh. Malaysia: Institute of Strategic and International Studies, 1992.

Gullick, J. M. *Malay Society in the Late Nineteenth Century: The Beginnings of Change*. Singapore: Oxford University Press, 1987.

Hew, C. S. "The Impact of Urbanization on Family Structure: The Experience of Sarawak, Malaysia". *SOJOURN* 18, no. 1 (2003): 89–109.

Humholtz, C. *Through Central Borneo*. Oxford: Oxford University Press, 1991.

Knapen, H. "Epidemics, Droughts, and Other Uncertainties in Southeast Borneo during the Eighteenth and Nineteenth Centuries". In *Paper Landscapes*, edited by P. Boomgard et al. Leiden: KITLV Press, 1997.

Lau, K. K. and S. Hardin. "Community Psychiatric Nursing: An Evaluation of Schizophrenic Patients in the First 3 Years". *Medical Journal of Malaysia* 51, no. 2 (1996): 242–54.

Manderson, L. *Sickness and the State, Health and Illness in Colonial Malaya 1870–1940*. Hong Kong: Cambridge University Press, 1996.

Mashman, V. "Warriors and Weavers: A Study of Gender Relations Among the Iban of Sarawak". In *Female and Male in Borneo: Contributions and Challenges to Gender Studies*, edited by V. H. Sutlive. Borneo Research Council Monograph Series. Shanghai, VA: Ashley Printing Services, 1987.

McCulloch, J. "The Theory and Practice of European Psychiatry in Colonial Africa". In *Colonialism and Psychiatry*, edited by D. Bhugra and R. Littlewood. Oxford: Oxford University Press, 2001.

Miles, A. *The Mentally Ill in Contemporary Society*. Oxford: Martin Robertson, 1981.

Nazroo, J. Y. *Ethnicity and Mental Health*. London: Policy Studies Institute, 1997.

Nieuwenhuis, A. "Ten Years of Hygiene and Ethnography in Primitive Borneo (1891–1901)". In *The Effect of Western Influence on Native Civilizations in the Malay Archipelago*, edited by B. Schrieke. Batavia: G. Kolff & Co., 1929.

Nissom, M. P. and K. E. Schmidt. "Land-Dayak Concept of Mental Illness'. *The Medical Journal of Malaya* XX1, no. 4 (1967): 352–57.

Osman, C. B. and O. Ainsah. "First Admissions to a Psychiatric Ward in a General Hospital". *Malaysian Journal of Psychiatry* 2 (1994): 21–26.

Prior, L. *The Social Organisation of Mental Illness*. London: Sage Publishers, 1993.

Ramli, H., et al. "A Prevalence Survey of Psychiatric Morbidity in a Rural Malaysian Village — A Preliminary Report". *Singapore Medical Journal* 6, no. 28 (1989): 530–33.

Ramon, S. *Mental Health in Europe: Ends, Beginnings and Rediscoveries*. Houndsmill, Basingstoke: MacMillan Press Ltd/MIND Publications, 1996.

Razali, S. M. "Psychiatrists and Folk Healers in Malaysia". *World Health Forum* 16 (1995): 56–58.

Razali, S. M., et al. "Belief in Supernatural Causes of Mental Illness among Malay Patients: Impact on Treatment". *ACTA Psychiatrica Scandinavica* 94 (1996): 229–33.

Razali, S. M. "Legitimizing Traditional Medicine: A Personal View". *Malaysian Psychiatry* 3, nos. 3/4 (1997): 72–74.

Rousseau, J. "Gender and Class in Central Borneo". In Sutlive, op. cit., 1991.

Russell, D. *Women, Madness and Medicine*. Cambridge: Polity Press, 1995.

Schmidt, K. E. "Management of Schizophrenia in Sarawak Mental Hospital, 1959". *Journal of Mental Science* 107 (1961): 157–60.

Schmidt, K. E. "Folk Psychiatry in Sarawak: A Tentative System of Psychiatry in the Iban". In *Magic, Faith and Healing*, edited by A. Kiev. New York: The Free Press, 1964.

Schneider, W. M. and Schneider, M. "Male/Female Distinction Among the Selako". In Sutlive, op. cit., 1991.

Showalter, E. "Victorian Women and Insanity". In *Madhouses, Mad Doctors and Madmen*, edited by A. Scull. London: The Athlone Press, 1981.

Teoh, Jin Inn. "History of Institutional Psychiatric Care in Singapore 1862–1967)". In *Psychological Problems and Treatment in Malaysia*, edited by Eng-Seong Tan and N. N. Wagner. Kuala Lumpur: University of Malaya Press, 1971.

Ussher, J. *Women's Madness: Misogyny or Mental Illness*. New York: Harvester Wheatsheaf, 1991.

Varma, S. L. and I. Sharma. Genetics of Schizophrenia — Implications for the Schizophrenia Spectrum Disorders. *Malaysian Journal of Psychiatry* 3, no. 2 (1995): 13–17.

Warner, R. "The Cultural Context of Mental Distress". In *Mental Health Matters*, edited by T. Heller et al. London: The Open University/ Macmillan Press, 1996.

Wetzel, J. W. "Women and Mental Health: A Global Perspective". *International Social Work* 43, no. 2 (April 2000): 205–15.

Yee, M. "Women Transmigrants in Malaysia: Identity, Work and the Household". *The Third Malaysian Studies Conference*. UKM Bangi, 6–8 August 2001.

5

Elderly Women's Experiences of Urbanization

Ling How Kee

Introduction

Accelerated urbanization in Sarawak in the last four decades has far reaching ramifications on the lives of people. The consequences of rural-urban migration such as changes in family structure, the breakdown of traditional support networks, advancement of technology, changes in communication networks and opportunities for employment have all been well documented. On the other hand, it needs to be noted that urbanization is not a uniform process, but a highly differentiated one. Firstly, state policies in Sarawak have seen a concentration of development in the urban centres, mainly in the major towns of Kuching, Sibu, Miri and later Bintulu. Secondly, the impact of urbanization is differently experienced by people in Sarawak not only as a result of this urban bias, but also because the impact of urbanization is mediated by class, ethnicity, gender and age.

How has urbanization impacted on women? What are the changes and adjustments that they have to make in their encounters with urbanization? Are they active agents or passive recipients? This chapter focuses on the lived experiences of elderly women in the urbanization process of Sarawak and examines how it has had an impact on them. Quantitative data presented aims to show key demographic characteristics of these women and whenever relevant, comparisons will be made to elderly men. Qualitative data based on in-depth interviews with several selected women were presented in the form of vignettes which sought to privilege their personal accounts of their journeys through the urbanization process. Drawing on both quantitative and qualitative data, emerging themes and issues are highlighted in the concluding section of this chapter.

Brief Background to the Study

Primary data in this chapter are drawn from a larger study, "Ageing in Sarawak: Needs, Impact and Emerging Issues", commissioned by the Ministry of Social Development and Urbanization, Sarawak. The main aim of this study was to examine demographic trends and assess the needs and emerging issues of the older population. The findings of the study would assist the state government in formulating policies and programmes for the elderly. The research team decided to use the government retirement age of 55 as the starting age for the definition of elderly persons. Such a starting age is also justified on the grounds that life expectancy in Malaysia, as in other developing countries, is shorter than in developed nations. According to estimates in 2004, the life expectancy for males is 69.29 years and for females is 74.81 years <www.epu.jpm.my>.

Three Divisional Administrative areas, namely Kuching, Sibu and Miri were chosen as the principal research sites. Within these sites, different regions — towns and villages — were selected in order to cover urban, semi-rural and rural settings. It included both women and men and people of different ethnic and socio-economic backgrounds. Based on a proportionate stratified sampling procedure, taking into consideration the total population in each district and division, 318 women out of a sample of 600 respondents were selected. In-depth interviews were conducted with elderly women and men, formal and informal carers to explore issues of concern. Excerpts from these interviews provided the vignettes for the discussion in this chapter.

Demographic Profile and Socio-economic Particulars of Elderly Women

First of all, it is relevant to highlight that despite the small sample of respondents, the study found a greater number of older women than men. Out of 22.7 per cent of respondents who were 75 years and above, the majority were women. What is interesting to note is that figures from the Sarawak Statistics Department showed that it was only in the 1990s that the number of elderly women began to exceed that of elderly men. In 1980, the male elderly population was marginally higher at 8.1 per cent compared to 8.0 per cent of female. In 1990, there were 8.8 per cent women compared to 8.0 per cent men aged 55 and above. This trend is increasing as can be seen in the figures for the year 2000, where the number of women has increased to 9.7 per cent as compared to 8.0 per cent of men. This is consistent with national figures. Tan and Masitah (1997) observed that prior to 1970, the lower number of elderly women compared to men is largely due to the higher female mortality as a result of high maternal mortality rate at that time. Since then, better medical and health services, specifically greater knowledge and availability in reproductive and maternal healthcare including access to family planning have enabled more women to live till old age.

Although the figure above seems to suggest that Sarawak may have been some twenty years behind compared to the national trend, it is apparent that Sarawak is experiencing the global trend of the feminization of ageing (ARROWs For Change 1999; Global Commission on Women's Health 1994). Given the dual trend of rapid urbanization and the feminization of ageing in Sarawak, it is therefore pertinent to explore these issues in this chapter.

1. Income

The respondents were asked about their total monthly income which included their spouses' income. From Figure 5.1, it is evident that most of the elderly women fall into the lower income group with a monthly income of less than RM200. The number of women having a monthly

FIGURE 5.1
Income per Month (including that of spouse)

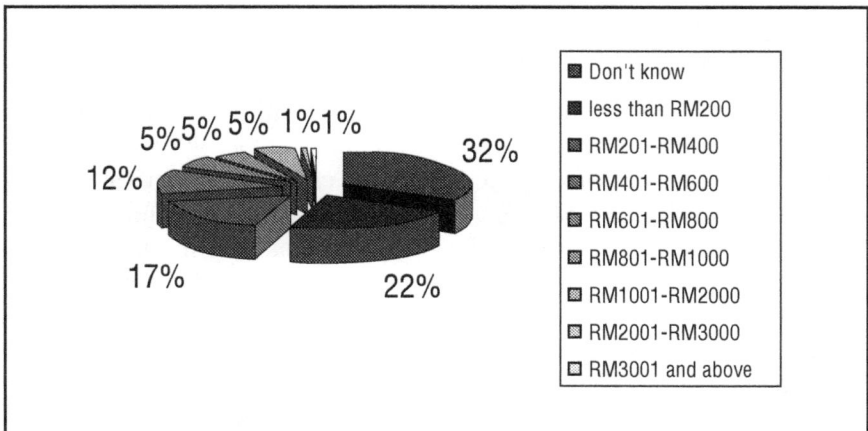

income which exceeded RM601 was significantly less than men. In addition, nearly 32 per cent of them (104) stated that they did not know their income as many did not receive any cash income which went directly to their husbands. This is in contrast to only 18 per cent (53) of men who said that they did not know their income. The low or lack of income of elderly women is indicative of their socio-economic status and their low participation rate in the formal employment sector which will be echoed in the employment section below.

2. Level of Education

The low monthly income of the women was a direct consequence of their lack of education as shown in Figure 5.2. Some 72 per cent of the elderly women in the study had no formal education as compared to only 31 per cent of elderly men. This is not surprising for women of their generation as parents at that time prioritized the education of sons over daughters.

FIGURE 5.2
Educational Level of Women and Men (per cent)

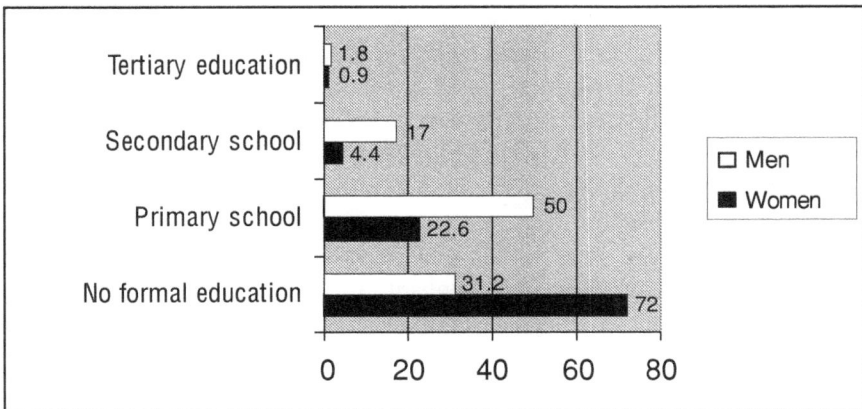

3. Employment: Previous and Current

When asked what their occupations were for most of their lives, nearly half of the total respondents (49 per cent) identified themselves as

FIGURE 5.3
Women's Previous Employment

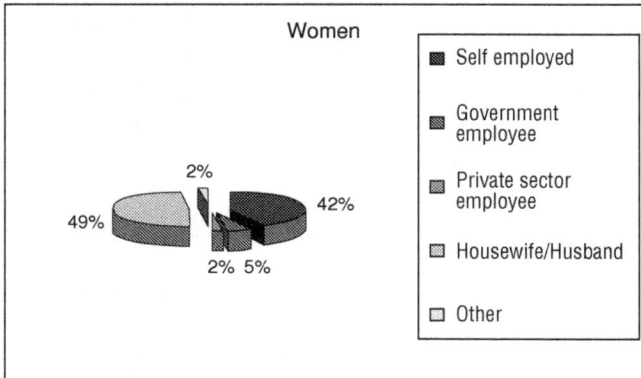

housewives followed closely by 42 per cent who said that they were self-employed. Of these self-employed groups, the common occupations mentioned were farmers, hairdressers, dressmakers and bakers. This shows that contrary to common perception that women of those eras were "just" housewives, a great many of them earned a living or supplemented their family income with agricultural or home-based businesses. This attested to the important contribution made by women to the economy of the household and the nation which has been largely undervalued and unrecognized (Hing and Rokiah Talib 1986; Jamilah Ariffin 1992).

Only 5 per cent of the elderly women interviewed had been employees in the government sector in comparison to 36 per cent of elderly men. This is largely due to the women's lack of formal education and no less, the male bias in government recruitment into the civil service. The figure in the private sector also depict a similar situation in which only 2 per cent of women were former employees compared to 10 per cent of men (Refer to Figure 5.4.)

Although the number of elderly women who had previously been employed is comparable to that of men, many more currently unemployed women are seeking paid work than men. At the time of the interview, 13 per cent (42) of the women were working full time while 4.4 per cent were seeking work. This suggests that employment opportunities for older women are more limited than that of older men.

FIGURE 5.4
Men's previous Employment

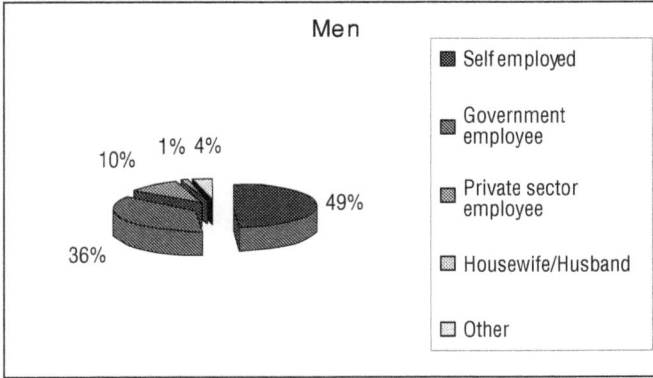

4. Social Roles and Community Participation

This question was designed to gauge the level of participation of the elderly people in the family and community. A significant number of women (20 per cent) said that they played an active role in caring for their grandchildren. This is translated directly from the term "*jaga cucu*" which literally means looking after grandchildren. This shows that grandmothers caring for grandchildren is still a common practice in Sarawak, although for those who are able to afford it, there is a growing trend in sending children to formal childcare centres in the urban areas. It is also noted that there were rural elderly women who were requested by their children to move to town to look after the grandchildren. This is particularly so in the case of younger couples who entered into the lower rungs of the job market who could not afford childcare services even with dual income, necessitating free "labour" of the elderly women. There are also others who left their children with their rural mothers while they worked in the urban sectors as in the case of some young single mothers discussed in Hew (2003). In this context, elderly women's role as *primary* caregiver to grandchildren and in turn facilitating younger women to enter or continue their participation in the formal workforce, is another area which warrants recognition.

While there has been "an explosion of interest" (Belsky 1999, p. 319) in Western literature in recent years on elderly women's grandparenting role in keeping the "more fragile younger family afloat" thus acting as safety net (ibid.), this has surprising not been so in the Malaysian context and certainly one worthy of future research. From this study, it appears that in some cases grandparenting role accords them a special position in their families, in others a sense of satisfaction and self-worth, while in others this role can be a source of stress and social restriction, as the vignettes in the later part of this chapter illustrate. It is also noteworthy that a further 24 per cent (76) of the elderly women see themselves as heads of the family (*ketua keluarga*) as their husbands have passed away.

In terms of community participation, more men (66 per cent) than women (47.5 per cent) said that they participated in one or more social, community or religious activities. It would therefore appear that women were more confined to home/family-based activities.

5. Living Arrangements and Level of Independence

Most of the women in this study lived with their spouses or children or an extended family. Only 4.2 per cent (25) women lived alone — out of which, 16 were from the rural areas and eight from urban areas while only one was from a semi-urban area. This is not surprising given the rapid rate of urbanization in Sarawak and the exodus of the young from villages leaving the old behind. However, it must also be pointed out that some of the elderly women interviewed chose to live alone. Good health and sound financial standing provided them with the social and economic independence to do so. A recent study in China showed that more and more elderly people are choosing to live on their own (Xiaolin Xie and Xia Yan 2001). With improved healthcare and better financial position, it may well become a future trend in Sarawak.

Poorly-educated elderly women from rural backgrounds face more obstacles than their more sophisticated urban counterparts in independent living. Illiteracy in the national language, modern systems of communication and transportation all pose formidable barriers for old village women living on their own. Longer life expectancy also meant that disability in their later years would further erode the independence of elderly women.

6. Health

The state of health of the women in this study was based on self-rating. About 52 per cent reported their health as good and a further 4 per cent said that their health was excellent. Further investigation of their use of medication and their responses to illnesses revealed that a substantial number of them suffered from one or several of the following: hypertension, heart disease, arthritis, hearing impairment and impaired vision particularly cataract, tuberculosis, and gastric problems. This finding is consistent with other studies done in different parts of Malaysia (Chen 1987*a*; Siop 2003; Tracy and Tracy 1993; Zaiton Yassin and Terry 1990).

In terms of mental health, some 63 per cent of the women interviewed reported symptoms of insomnia, loneliness, depression and anxiety. Although the scope of this study did not permit a further analysis as to whether this can be attributed to the alienating effects of urbanization, several points can be observed from further exploration on a number of case studies. First, isolation and loneliness for some women are closely related to the loosening of family and social support network as a result of rural-urban migration of their children. Second, health (including mental health) and poverty is a vicious circle — poverty increases health problems and those with health problems are at risk of falling into poverty. The vulnerability of elderly women from the lower income group to poor health is compounded by the inaccessibility of healthcare in the rural areas (Chen 1987*b*; Teoh, Rosdinom Razali and Normah Che Din 2001). Third, loneliness and depression is a vicious circle; and of particular concern was that 7 per cent said that they had no one to turn to when they had personal or emotional problems.

Thus the health indicators for elderly women are mixed. As noted earlier, better maternal healthcare have improved women's health and life expectancy. However, geriatric healthcare has not developed in tandem with the increased demand of an ageing population, and this will have greater implications for elderly women than men because of their longer life expectancy and lower economic position.

The demographic characteristics of the elderly women as outlined above give us a glimpse of elderly women in Sarawak. Their situations echo what has been reported by the United Nations Economic and Social Commission for Asia and the Pacific (UNESCAP 1991, p. 26): "... the growing number of elderly women [in this region] is ... associated with high widowhood status, low labour force participation rates, low level of education and lower health status".

First, we noted that women's life expectancy is becoming longer, surpassing that of men. This, however, means that the proportion of the remaining years that are disability free is less than that of men. Second, these women had not had the same educational and employment opportunities as their male counterparts and as the women of today. This social disadvantage is reflected in their low labour participation rate throughout their lives, as well as low or even the lack of income for many of them. Thus, feminization of poverty in a developing region like Sarawak (Jamiliah Ariffin 1994) is thus accentuated in old age. Third, the traditional sex role of women as homemakers and caregivers made them convenient childminders for their grandchildren. In many instances, this is necessitated by the participation of their daughters or daughter-in-laws in the workforce — partly a result of urbanization. Yet there is indication that family care and traditional support network is either diminishing or no longer able to provide the social and emotional security needed for the later years of the women's life-course. Neither are supportive services for healthcare and mental health developed to meet the needs of many of the elderly women. Some of these themes are amplified when these women's experiences are further explored, based on the qualitative data obtained through in-depth interviews.

Elderly Women's Experiences of Urbanization

In the following sections, thematic discussions of the different life situations and experiences of elderly women are presented through illustrative vignettes. To ensure anonymity, pseudonyms are used and names of the villages where they lived have been withheld. The titles in front of their names indicate the local ways of addressing older women often in accordance with their age: *Kak* is sister, *Mak* is auntie, *Nek* is grandma. *Puan* or Madam are respectful title for a married woman.

Urban Elderly Women

1. Madam Siew Lan

Elderly women with sound financial support like Madam Siew Lan, a 69-year-old Chinese, are able to tap into the modern amenities and infrastructure in urban centres for greater social networks and better healthcare. Madam Siew Lan was educated up to junior secondary school. A homemaker for most of her life, she lives with her husband and married children in the centre of Sibu. Besides her five children and thirty-one grandchildren, she has a close support network through the local Methodist Church where she has been active since her teens. Living in a fast developing town, she is well informed of the availability of health services through her social networks. Financially, she is well supported by her husband and children and this has enabled her to enjoy good healthcare. She suffered from cataracts a few years ago and has undergone surgery once. At the time of the interview, she was scheduled for another surgery and was very optimistic of the outcome.

2. Mrs Teo

For some women like Mrs Teo, a 63-year-old retired primary school teacher, her golden years has brought independence and freedom. Her husband and two married children migrated to Australia several years ago. However, she chose to live alone in her doubled-storey house in the city of Miri. She enjoys gardening, exercising, reading and watching television — activities which she could not do while employed and parenting in her younger days. Although she experiences loneliness at times, life is generally interesting and exciting. She owns a car and enjoys full autonomy and freedom of movement. She travels to Australia several times a year to be with her family and to have a break from being "home alone". With a pension of RM2,000.00 a month, Mrs Teo said she has more than enough to meet her needs.

3. *Kak* Rahmah

For women like Madam Siew Lan and Mrs Teo who are from a relatively higher socio-economic strata, they are able to take full advantage of facilities and opportunities that come with urbanization. For 57-year-old *Kak* Rahmah, who was widowed seven years ago, the benefits are not so clear cut. She lives with one of her married son and grandchildren in a residential area twenty-minutes' drive from the capital city of Kuching. Financially, she relies on her late husband's pension of RM400.00 a month and her son's monthly allowance of RM50.00.

In the last twenty years, rapid urbanization has transformed the sleepy village where she grew up into a modern residential suburb. The nearest shop is only a five-minute walk away. It takes another five minutes to walk to the nearest bus stop for a bus to the city. *Kak* Rahmah is an active member of a political party and she is also a committee member in her local mosque. Although urbanization has made her life more comfortable, she feels ambivalent about the advantages of living in the city.

She recounted her days when as a young mother she had to work hard to make ends meet. Her husband's salary as a junior government employee was not enough to meet the expenses of a family of four children. She had to supplement his income by making and selling fish cakes (*keropok lekor*). Her hard work has paid off as all her adult children are now gainfully employed. However, the higher cost of living in the city meant that they also had to work extra hard to make ends meet. She lamented the hectic life of her children and grandchildren and was nostalgic for the slow-paced village life in days gone by.

While *Kak* Rahmah had to adjust to an urban way of life as urbanization engulfed the village where she grew up, others plunged into city life when they followed their children as they migrated to the urban areas. While some made an easy transition, others lose their autonomy and become more dependent on their families.

Migrant Elderly Women

1. *Mak* Salema

Mak Salema, a 73-year-old Iban from a longhouse in a sub-district of Sibu, moved to Miri a few years ago with her 10-year-old grandson and they live in a low-cost housing estate. Her youngest son (the father of this grandchild) is divorced and was given custody of his child. He has since remarried and had migrated to Kuala Lumpur for employment and only returns to see his mother and son once a year. Fortunately for *Mak* Salema, she has two other sons living in the same housing estate whom she relies on for support.

Migration from a traditional rural longhouse to an urban housing estate has made a huge impact on *Mak* Salema's life. As an elderly rural migrant to the city, *Mak* Salema has adjusted well to living in Miri. She is very independent and has learnt to use the mobile phone. She is also familiar with public transportation which she frequently uses. Presently, she does not have any financial difficulties as her son sends her up to RM1,000 per month. She keeps herself busy with gardening and visiting her sons. She is in good health and only has moderate gastric problems and poor eyesight to worry about.

2. *Mak* Martha

The contrast between *Mak* Salema and *Mak* Martha cannot be greater. Both are in their 70s and rural migrant grandmothers, but *Mak* Martha, a

71-year-old Kenyah woman did not fare as well. When her husband passed away two years ago, *Mak* Martha reluctantly migrated from her small village in Marudi to live with one of her married sons in Miri. As both her son and daughter-in-law are at work during the day, she has to look after her four-year-old grandson. Although she is independent within the confines of the home, it is a different story when it comes to outside activities. She is totally dependent on others in the use of modern technology such as a telephone. Using public transportation like getting on a bus is a struggle for her. She feels alienated in a hectic urban environment like Miri and misses the peace and calm of her village. Her only enjoyment is when she walks up to an hour with some friends like herself to the nearest jungle to pick wild ferns (*paku-pakis*). Picking wild ferns gives her a sense of being back in the village where she feels she belongs.

3. *Puan* Ruth

Still worse is the experience of *Puan* Ruth, a 74-year-old widow from one of the Orang Ulu communities. Her case is one of elder abuse, an issue which is very much hidden in Malaysian society (Abdul Razak and Abd. Manaf 2002). She migrated from her remote village to stay with her son and daughter-in-law in Miri. She finds her daughter-in-law intimidating and was told not to leave the house and socialize with the neighbours. Neglected by them, she had to prepare her own food and do her own laundry. A helpful neighbour gave her some clothes and a *sarong* but her own family did not provide her with any. When she wanted to return to the village and live alone, her daughter-in-law stopped her son from giving her money for that purpose. *Puan* Ruth also wanted more of her regular medicine but her family has not attended to this. She has high blood pressure, backache, "nerve pain" and coughs up blood.

These are some of the stories of those who followed their children in their migration from village to town but how is life for those who stayed behind? We will now turn our attention to elderly women in rural areas.

Rural Elderly Women

1. *Mak* Nisah

Mak Nisah, a 76-year-old Malay woman who stays alone at a small village 40 kilometres from Miri since her husband's death ten years ago, typifies the forgotten ones in the face of urbanization. *Mak* Nisah's two married sons found employment in Miri and settled there. She has hardly any contact with them and do not even remember the last time they visited. Neither does she have any idea how many grandchildren she has. Her younger sister who lives nearby is her only source of help in times of need. She receives a meagre sum of RM100 a month from the Welfare Department under the Elderly Persons Assistance Scheme (*Bantuan Orang Tua*) and some support in the form of food and kind from the local community especially during major festivals. She suffers from high blood pressure, a circulation problem in arms and legs and haemorrhoids. She requires supportive devices such as spectacles, walking cane and dentures. She also needs home assistance in all her daily activities but these kinds of services have yet to be introduced by the state to reach out to the elderly. Life in old age for *Mak* Nisah is one of sadness and loneliness. At the time of interview, she could not hold back tears as she recounted her destiny.

2. *Nek* Tumah

The uneven pace of development in the state meant that some elderly women are affected more while others much less by the differential rate of urbanization. *Nek* Tumah, a 87-year-old Bidayuh woman widowed seven years ago, lived with her son and a daughter-in-law in a small village 15 kilometres from Kota Pedawan which is a satellite bazaar, 16 kilometres from Kuching. Although wheelchair-bound, she enjoyed close family ties, being regularly visited by her other children and grandchildren who lived in the same village. She was active in village activities in her younger days and recalled them with much pride.

Although there was been rapid physical development in her village in more recent years as a result of accelerated development in Kota Pedawan, this does not seem to have a direct impact on *Nek* Tumah's life. She seldom left the village and the occasional trip to Kota Pedawan was mainly to seek medical treatment from a doctor.

3. *Nek* Siew Mei

Another elderly woman living in the fringes of urbanization is *Nek* Siew Mei, an 80-year-old Chinese woman from a village near the small town of Niah which is 109 kilometres from Miri. Although Niah is accelerating in its development, *Nek* Siew Mei's little village is neglected. She has two children and five grandchildren. She stays with her husband, her youngest married son and four grandchildren in a shophouse. They owned a grocery shop which is now managed by her son. Her other son owns a furniture shop in Miri. She disclosed that she led an uninteresting life as her daughter-in-law has taken over her domestic responsibilities. In a village with less than ten shophouses, there was not much to do. She spends most of her days at a nearby shop and "hangs out" with friends of her own age. *Nek* Siew Mei complains of lower back pain, gout and circulation problem in her arms and legs. She too has undergone an operation for her cataract problem.

Conclusion

It is evident from this study that the impact of urbanization on women are different. For some women, it has brought greater opportunities including educational facilities and employment in their younger days, and better health care in their old age. For others, urbanization has been detrimental to their well-being. The vignettes above point to the fact that those who have some education and can enjoy a measure of economic independence are those who have a better experience of ageing. However, many elderly women in Sarawak are likely to be in the lower socio-economic strata as this cohort of women did not have the same educational and employment opportunities as their male counterparts, unlike the women of today. Thus many elderly women become socially and economically dependent on their children.

In the context of rapid urbanization in Sarawak, this dependence translates to migration in their old age where women move in with their city-dwelling children. This requires drastic adjustments on their part. While some are able to cope, others fail miserably. Those left behind in the villages experience neglect if they live alone. In spite of such differences, one thing is clear. Those who are able to maintain close family ties and have a strong support network outside are able to offset the alienating effects of urbanization and are better cared for even in the rural areas, as in the case of *Nek* Tumah and *Nek* Siew Mei.

Another pertinent issue raised in this study is that of a need for an alternative system of eldercare. As a result of a longer female life expectancy, many of the women interviewed would have taken care of their ailing spouses. However, when their turn comes for receiving care, traditional caregivers such as daughters and daughters-in-law are no longer available. With urbanization and expanded employment opportunities, more and more women are entering the workforce and the elderly are left at home not only to fend for themselves but also frequently have childcare thrust upon them, as in the case of *Mak* Martha. Depending on their health status and the presence of other support networks, this may, for some, be enhancing their social role but for others, a burden.

The impact of urbanization on elderly women has pointed to several important concerns which urgently require policy responses. Among these are the need for income support, for strengthening family and community care, for preventative and rehabilitative geriatric healthcare services, for elderly-friendly housing and facilitation environment. These policy responses need to incorporate a gender perspective besides addressing specific needs of rural elders.

The experiences of elderly women in this study have given us insights into how they lived with urbanization. Each is a story of a woman's personal journey — engaging with social changes, with life's opportunities and confronting one's own vulnerability. Their role and participation in the urbanization process must be highlighted, and their contribution in the society should be equally acknowledged as that of men, so should opportunities, for community participation and self-fulfilment be promoted. It is hoped that the experiences of elderly women highlighted in this chapter would increase awareness of their needs (Mehta 1997), that their voices are heard and their dignity respected.

Acknowledgement

I wish to acknowledge the Ministry of Social Development and Urbanization, Sarawak for their permission to publish the findings of the study in this chapter and for the work of team researchers in this study — Spencer Empading, Gill Raja and Zuraidah Abdul Rahman.

References

Abdul Razak B. Abd. Manaf. *Penderaan Warga Tua: Masalah yang Tersembunyi*. In Abdul Razak Abd Manaf and Zakiyah Jamaluddin, *Kerja Sosial: Artikel-Artikel Pilihan*, Kuala Lumpur: Utusan Publications, 2002.

ARROWs For Change. "Feminization of Aging in Asia-Pacific: Health Implications", 5, no. 2 (1999): 12.

Belsky, J. *The Psychology of Ageing: Theory, Research and Intervention*. Pacific Grove, California: Brooks/Cole Publishing Company, 1999, 3rd edition.

Chen, P. C. Y. "The Health of the Aging Malaysian: Policy Implications". *Medical Journal of Malaysia*, 42, no. 3 (1987*a*): 146–55.

———. "Psychosocial Factors and the Health of the Elderly Malaysian". *Annals of the Academy of Medicine*, Singapore, 16, no. 1 (1987*b*): 10–14.

Global Commission on Women's Health. "Women's Health: Towards a Better World". Initial Issues Paper. Geneva: World Health Organization (WHO), 1994.

Hew, Cheng Sim. "The Impact of Urbanization on Family Structures: The Experience of Sarawak, Malaysia". *SOJOURN* 8, no. 1 (2003): 110–38.

Hing, Ai Yun and Rokiah Talib, ed. *Women and Work in Malaysia*. Department of Anthropology and Sociology, University of Malaya, University of Malaya Women's Association, the Asia and Pacific Development Centre, 1986.

Jamilah, Ariffin. *Women and Development in Malaysia*. Petaling Jaya: Pelanduk Publications, 1992.

Jamilah, Ariffin, ed. *Poverty Amidst Plenty*. Petaling Jaya: Pelanduk Publications, 1994.

Mehta, Kalyani, ed. Untapped Resources: Women in Ageing Societies Across *Asia*. Singapore: Time Academic Press, 1997.

Siop, S. *Health Needs of Older People in a Semi-urban Village in Malaysia*. Kota Samarahan: Universiti Malaysia Sarawak, 2003.

Tan, Poo Chang and Masitah Mohd. Yatim. "Old Age Financial Security for Women in Malaysia". In *Untapped Resources: Women in Ageing Societies Across Asia*, edited by Mehta, Kalyani. Singapore: Time Academic Press, 1997.

Teoh, Hsien-Jin, Rosdinom Razali and Normah Che Din. *Mental Health of the Malaysian Elderly: Issues and Perspectives in Mental Health in Malaysia*, edited by Amber Haque. Kuala Lumpur: UM Press, 2001.

Tracy, M. B. and P. D. Tracy. "Health Care and Family Support System of Functionally Impaired Rural Elderly Men and Women in Trengganu, Malaysia". *Journal of Cross-cultural Gerontology* 8 (1993): 35–48.

United Nations Economic and Social Commission for Asia and the Pacific (UNESCAP). "Status of Elderly Women in Asia and the Pacific Region". Bangkok: UNESCAP, 1991.

Xie, Xiaolin and Xia Yan. "Adult Children Taking Care of their Ageing Parents: A Multiple-case Study on Caregivers Perspectives". *International Social Work* 11, no. 2 (2001): 52–64.

Zaiton, Yassin and R. D. Terry. "Health Characteristics of Rural Elderly Malay Females in Selected Villages in Negeri Sembilan". *Medical Journal of Malaysia* 45, no. 4 (1990), 310–18.

6

Like a Chicken Standing on One Leg
Urbanization and Single Mothers[1]

Hew Cheng Sim

"Like a chicken standing on one leg (*saperti ayam berdiri satu kaki*)". This was the comment given by one woman when asked how she would describe her single motherhood. This chapter shines the torch on the experiences of single mothers both rural and urban, and examines the problems that they face and the support networks that exist to assist them. The discussion also includes the profile of their marriages and the causes of marital fragmentation.

Changes in Family Form: A Discussion

The family has been a subject of much theorizing and many of the arguments are well known. Although reviewing these theories is not the primary aim of this chapter, nevertheless, it is useful to contextualize the discussion on debates about the family.

At a global level, the rise in female-headed households is one of the most important recent changes in the structure of household and family. It has been estimated that female-headed households account for a third of all urban households in Asia, Latin America and parts of Africa (Pearson 1994 in Hewitt, Johnson and Wield 1994, p. 245). Debates about the family have often been defined by two opposing positions. On one side are those who argue that current changes in the structure of the family is not a new phenomenon but that from time to time, changes have been seen in the family structure as it adapts to changed circumstances. The other camp believes that the current changes are a consequence of an irreversible breakdown in values. Those who argue the former include a wide spectrum of perspectives. The Chicago School of Sociology, for instance, looked at the consequences of urbanization on family structure in post-World War I America. Researchers in the Chicago School wrote of the alienating and disintegrating forces of urbanization on the family where the extended family fragmented into nuclear families, where rootlessness replaced support structures of old kinship networks.

Another perspective that also examines changes in the family in the context of wider societal change is functionalism. Talcott Parson's concept of institutional differentiation as a result of modernization argued that functions that were formerly performed by the family, for example, the education of children, the care of the sick and economic production have now been taken over by other institutions in society. Thus, the family has new functions and the central responsibilites of the family have changed (Berger and Berger 1992). However, writers like Fletcher (in Bilton et al. 1987, p. 263) have objected to the view that the taking over of the family's functions by commercial agencies and state organizations has eroded it as an institution. Instead, Fletcher argued that the multi-functional pre-industrial family is a myth. His view is that, in the first place, the harsh realities of life in the pre- and early industrial period meant that the family performed minimally in education and care of the sick.

The Marxists, on the other hand, linked their analysis to the changes in the mode of production. Wally Seccombe (1993), for instance, argued that family forms and the mode of production are closely enmeshed, and the transformation of the former will follow closely on the heels of the latter. In other words, a certain mode of production will facilitate the reproduction of a certain family form while impeding the development of others. When discussing the changing family form during the first and second industrial revolutions in Europe, he pointed out that the capitalist mode of production severed the bonds between adult children and their parents. This was because the individuated wage could not sustain anything more than a nuclear family of parents and their children. Those who did not stand to inherit any productive property or a father's trade had to sell their labour as free workers in the labour market. Thus, the young left home to find employment, spent their wages as they like, married a spouse of their own choice and lived wherever they could afford.

The opposing view that changes in the structure of the family has been caused by an irreversible breakdown in values has been taken on board by the Malaysian media, politicians and policymakers. Hence, the 1.1 per cent of the female population who are single mothers has captured the attention of the nation. The flurry of activity and discussion which accompanied the "discovery" of single mothers in Malaysia must be seen in the context of the moral panics of the 1990s, where a whole myriad of social "problems" concerning women, adolescents and the family were highlighted in the media and involved various government agencies. These social "problems" included teenagers loafing in shopping complexes, known as "*lepak*", teenagers soliciting free sex — "*bohsia*" for women (literally means "no noise" in the Hokkien dialect) and "*bohjan*" for men (composite word "*boh*" meaning "no/none" in Hokkien and "*jan*" from "*jantan*" the Malay word for males). This of course leads to the next "problem" of illegitimate babies that are abandoned in dustbins. The gendered nature of these moral panics merits an entire study of its own. However, it suffices to say here that the position which suggests that the rise in single motherhood and female headed households are due to a decline in moral values is difficult to sustain.

First, significant numbers of women are widowed rather than divorced and in many parts of the world this has been due to wars. Second, the unprecedented rate of migration and urbanization meant that women and men are moving to where the jobs are. In recent years, there has been a rise in female migration as employment opportunities for women increase at a faster rate than men's. Women not only migrate to the urban areas but also to other countries. This is particularly so in the Asia-Pacific region where the transmigration of women is a well-studied phenomenon (Salaff 2002; Heyzer 1989).

It is important to note also that female headship is not a recent phenomenon but that it has been observed in different countries in different historical epochs. One example of the rise in female headship as a result of rapid economic change is that due to slavery and colonization. In the mid-eighteenth century Caribbean, the desire of slave owners to reproduce labour led to a promotion of high female fertility rates outside of marriage. Hence, common law marriages were typical amongst black and mestizo populations and many children were born out of wedlock and a large percentage of households were female headed (Moore 1994, p. 9).

Although it is important to remember that female headship could be due to many causes, it is equally significant that it could pass through different phases in its life-cycle. For example, a woman may decide to remarry. Conversely, in the context of Sarawak, migration, divorce, widowhood and abandonment may not result in female-headed households as many women return to live with their parents, siblings and other kin from their natal families. Thus, the analysis of families and households are very much linked to an understanding of life phases, use of labour and marital and survival strategies.

Another confusion which often arise in any discussion of the family is the conflation of family with household. Recruitment into the household is not only through kinship and marriage but also through adoption, domestic service, temporary residential sharing and purchase. Thus, household and family are not necessarily the same thing. There could be several family units in a household and conversely, family members could spread over several households. Different family members have very different experiences of family life depending on their positions in the life-course and hence their differing roles and expectations.

The diversity of family forms has therefore existed not only in different cultures but also historically over time. Even individual families will pass through different forms at different stages of their development. In other words, anthropological and historical studies have demonstrated that throughout history, there has been no single trajectory of change in family form.

Although social transformations and its consequences on family form have long been studied elsewhere, in the context of Sarawak, rapid urbanization in the previous decades meant that it is only now that the multi-faceted impact of rural-urban migration has become topics of urgent investigation.

How the Term Single Mother [*Ibu Tunggal*] is Used in Malaysia

As mentioned earlier, single motherhood was "discovered" as a social phenomenon in Malaysia in the late 1990s. The Malaysian use of the term "single mothers" or *ibu tunggal* needs some clarification. Single mothers include women who are young unwed mothers, those who widowed, divorced/separated, abandoned by their partners [*digantung tidak bertali*, which literally means "hanging without a rope"] and unmarried women who adopted children. In addition, women head of households (those with ill or absent partners) are also included in the ambit of the term *ibu tunggal*. In the year 2000 in Malaysia, there were 130,249 single mothers who consituted 1.1 per cent of the female population (Department of Statistics, Malaysia 2000).

Single Mothers in Sarawak

Sarawak, with 8,011 single mothers, ranked nineth highest in terms of the number of single mothers amongst all the thirteen states and two federal territories. However, in the total number of civil divorces from 1982–2000, Sarawak ranked fourth in the highest number of divorces in the country after Kuala Lumpur, Pahang and Pulau Pinang in that order (*Jabatan Pendaftaran Negara*). It has to be pointed out that the figures for civil divorce and marriage did not include the majority of the indigenous population in Sarawak who marry and divorce through customary laws [*adat*]. Unfortunately, statistics for divorce through native customary *adat* are not available. In the period 1991–2000, the ratio of Muslim divorce to marriage in Sarawak was 10.3 per cent while the ratio for civil divorce to marriage in the state stood at only 2.3 per cent (*Jabatan Kemajuan Islam Malaysia*).[2]

The Women's Bureau, Ministry of Social Development and Urbanization in Sarawak was instructed by HAWA (Women's Affairs Unit in the Prime Minister's Department) to conduct a survey on single mothers in the state in May 1999. The survey opened up a Pandora's box which led to much public discussion and debate. Although the subject of single mothers and their plight generated much interest amongst politicians and the public at large, there was little information but much speculation. At the end of 2000, the Ministry of Social Development and Urbanization in Sarawak commissioned a study to better understand the position of single mothers in the state. It is on the findings of this study that this chapter is based.

About the Study[3]

The brief given for the research was that the information collected should be useful for formulating programmes and policies to assist needy single mothers. Thus, it was decided that only single mothers without tertiary education would be included in the investigation. The study included 231 single mothers from ten geographical locations throughout Sarawak. A total of 52.8 per cent were from the urban areas and the rest were from the rural areas. In addition, 29 per cent were Malays, 27 per cent Ibans, 26 per cent Bidayuh, 13 per cent Chinese and the rest were Orang Ulu. The marital profile of the respondents included 60 per cent who were either divorced or undergoing divorce, 12 per cent who were separated from their partners and husbands, 14 per cent who were unwed mothers and 14 per cent who were widowed. The respondents were all aged below fifty and had dependent children. The average age of the respondents was 37 years. Respondents had an average of three children and 34 per cent of them had children below six years of age.

The research consisted of two parts. First a quantitative aspect examined their profile, that of their relationships, causes for the fragmentation of relationships and problems faced. These aspects were analysed in terms of their urban/rural location and ethnicity. The second aspect of the study was qualitative and ethnographic in nature. This is because the complexity of women's experiences and the multi-faceted nature of their lives are not easily quantifiable. Construction of closed categories in quantitative surveys restricted analysis to only those given categories, and matters outside the ambit of those categories are considered exceptions, irregular and therefore ignored. Qualitative ethnographies, on the other hand, places women's experiences centre-stage. Complexities and contradictions are not smoothed away but restored and grounded. In this way, the multi-dimensionality of women's lives is captured. Thus, the research findings relevant to this chapter are presented both quantitatively and qualitatively and specific cases are used to illustrate a point. All names used in this chapter are pseudonyms.

Rural and Urban Single Mothers: A Comparison

1. Education and Employment

As a result of their remote geographical location, rural single mothers often had very little schooling. Many were either illiterate or had only a primary school education in comparison to their urban counterparts. Chinese respondents who mainly resided in urban centres received the most education while their Bidayuh sisters in the villages had the least schooling. Table 6.1 below shows the educational attainment of respondents by location.

Given that there are greater employment opportunities in urban centres and given the poor educational status of rural single mothers, it is not surprising that there were marginally more unemployed single mothers in the rural areas than the urban areas. A quarter of Malay and non-Muslim indigenous single mothers was unemployed in comparison to only ten per

TABLE 6.1
Educational Attainments of Respondents by Location

Location	Educational Attainment of Respondents			
	No schooling and primary school	Secondary school	Tertiary education	Total
Urban	51 (42%)	68 (56%)	3 (2%)	122 (100%)
Rural	58 (53%)	51 (47%)	–	109 (100%)

cent of Chinese single mothers. Table 6.2 shows the distribution of unemployed single mothers within ethnicity.

Even when they are employed, rural single mothers worked in the agricultural sector which pays much poorer wages than those of their urban sisters who are more likely to work in the service sectors. Many rural single mothers worked as paddy farmers, market gardeners and plantation workers and earned less than RM300 a month, while urban single mothers frequently had multiple jobs and earned more. Table 6.3 shows the break-down in the income ranges of rural and urban single mothers.

TABLE 6.2
Unemployed Single Mothers within Ethnicity

Ethnicity of single mothers	No. of unemployed single mothers (%)
Malay	18 (26.5%)
Iban	17 (27.4%)
Bidayuh	13 (21.3%)
Chinese	3 (10%)
Others	2 (20%)

TABLE 6.3
Income Ranges and Locations of Single Mothers

Location	Income ranges of single mothers in RM[4]					Total
	<300	301–600	601–900	901–1200	>1200	
Urban	52 (48%)	29 (27%)	12 (11%)	10 (9%)	5 (5%)	108 (100%)
Rural	81 (76%)	17 (16%)	8 (8%)	–	–	106 (100%)

Examples of the multiple jobs held by single mothers included one respondent who reared chickens for sale, did tailoring and was employed in a foodstall. Another single mother was a cleaner, did laundry and child-sat for others. One single mother in Miri worked as a clerk and pressed sugarcane juice for sale to coffee shops for an extra income. Yet another single mother in Kuching was a hairdresser, tailor and reflexologist. Another study participant was a cleaner and a coffee-shop assistant. Some 71 per cent of those employed at the time of the interview were in full-time employment, 10 per cent were in part-time employment and 19 per cent were in both types of employment. In addition, urban single mothers often have a longer employment history and have done more jobs (as many as eight different jobs) than rural single mothers. More respondents in the urban areas mentioned landing jobs from advertisements in newspapers and seeking out potential employers directly while their rural counterparts are more likely to be introduced by friends and relatives.

2. Support Networks

The majority of nuclear households were to be found in the urban centres while extended households were more frequent in the rural areas. The only ethnic group living more in nuclear households than extended ones was the Chinese. It was therefore not surprising that the Chinese were the second largest group who said that they did not have any support networks (after the Malay). Rural single mothers had greater support from parents and grandparents while more of their urban sisters either did not have any support networks or else relied more on their friends and neighbours rather than kin.

In other words, urban single mothers had greater difficulties in obtaining childcare than their rural counterparts who, in the main, lived in longhouses. The main reason for a lack of childcare was because the majority of urban single mothers had migrated from their hometowns and therefore lived away from their natal families. Their main reasons for migration were employment and marriage. Amongst the fifty respondents who migrated from their home towns, slightly more than half (52 per cent or 26) migrated as single women in search of employment. Others followed their husbands or fathers when the latter were transferred on work. Table 6.4 and 6.5 shows the number of nuclear and extended households by location and ethnicity respectively.

However, it would be wrong to assume that all single mothers living

TABLE 6.4
Number of Nuclear and Extended Households by Location

Location	Nuclear households	Extended households	Total
Urban	45 (37%)	77 (63%)	122 (100%)
Rural	23 (21%)	86 (79%)	109 (100%)

TABLE 6.5
Number of Nuclear and Extended Households by Ethnicity

Ethnicity of respondents	Nuclear households	Extended households	Total
Malay	23 (34%)	45 (66%)	68 (100%)
Chinese	18 (60%)	12 (40%)	30 (100%)
Bidayuh	13 (21%)	48 (79%)	61 (100%)
Iban	10 (16%)	52 (84%)	62 (100%)
Others	4 (40%)	6 (60%)	10 (100%)

in extended families or in villages will necessarily have support networks. The case of Sharifah from an urban area and Hayati from a rural setting illustrate the diversity of circumstances of the single mothers interviewed.

Both Sharifah and Hayati met younger men at age 18 and had their first baby at 19. Sharifah's husband had an extra-marital affair and both women were abused by their husbands. Sharifah is divorced now but Hayati's divorce is still pending. Both are now in their twenties and live with their parents in large households consisting of thirteen persons in each.

Sharifah is an Iban who converted to Islam through marriage. She is 27 years old and has a son who is in Primary Two. She lives with her parents who are both farmers in Lundu. Her household consists of her parents, her eldest sister and her brother-in-law and two of their children, brother number five, his wife and two of their children and of course, Sharifah and her son. Sharifah, who has completed Form Three, holds down two jobs — one in the day as a sales assistant in a shop selling baby clothes and at night, as an assistant at a foodstall. She earns RM340 a month from her day job and RM5 a night from the stall. In other words, her total monthly income is RM490. She is able to work day and night as her sister and sister-in-law do all the domestic chores and look after her son. Her brother-in-law and brother number five share the food and household bills and she is able to save some money every month. As they are already so supportive, she is reluctant to burden them further if she should need money for some emergency. She said that, in an emergency, she will get a loan from her employer who will deduct payment from her wages. She said, "*Kalau terlalu desak, pinjam dari towkay, potong gaji kelak. Si pernah minta dari rumah.*"

Although Hayati's household is as large as Sharifah's, her circumstances are very different. She is 23 years old and has two children. Her father died when she was very young and her mother remarried a man twenty years older. She has eleven half brothers and sisters. Her household consists of her stepfather, her mother, Hayati and one of her children (aged three), and nine other brothers and sisters aged between two to seventeen. As they are all still studying, they are not of much help to her. Between Hayati and her mother, they do most of the household chores and look after her sick stepfather. Although Hayati has completed Form Five, she works in an oil palm estate in Simunjan for RM12 a day. A day without work is a day without pay. She explained that it is extremely hardwork at the estate. "I am small in build and the work is heavy. My body always aches because I have to carry heavy sacks of fertilizer. [*Saya tubuh kecil dan kerja itu sangat berat. Badan saya selalu sakit kerana mengangkat guni baja.*]"

She has nobody to depend on and said that she would borrow from friends when in a very tight spot. In fact, life has been so difficult that she was forced to give the younger of her two children for adoption. Her mother too had given a daughter and a son for adoption.

3. Marriages and Relationships

Generally, the women in this study met their partners very young, when they were between 19–20 years old and had their first baby by the time they were 22. Rural single mothers were almost twice as likely to have had arranged marriages than their urban sisters, who frequently met their partners at their places of work, during a celebration [*kenduri/gawai*][5] or through friends and relatives. The case of Agnes below is an illustration of an arranged marriage at a young age in the village [*kampung*]. It also shows that urbanization and labour migration to the urban centres are important factors in fragmenting families and marriages.

At age 18, Agnes' grandfather arranged for her to marry a Bidayuh from another *kampung*. He was a construction worker, a year older than her. The marriage lasted sixteen years. The eldest son is 14 years old and the twin boys are a year younger. When she had only one child, she used to stay with him in different construction sites in Kuching. When she had the twins, she returned to stay in the village to farm. When her husband broke up with her, he dug up a hundred pepper posts,[6] sold them and kept the money for himself. He left them nothing and did not pay any maintenance. He later married a woman from his own village. That relationship also did not work out and he is currently with his third wife in Padawan. One night in 2001, he kidnapped the twins to Padawan[7] and it took Agnes, with help from fellow villagers, a few days to locate them in Padawan.

Similarly, Rina's parents arranged for her to marry another Bidayuh who was a construction worker. They had a customary marriage in the village and it lasted for three years. When their daughter was born, he was caught with a Malay woman [*tangkap basah*] and he decided to marry her.[8] He was nowhere to be found but Rina continued to hope that he would come back one day.

The most frequently mentioned cause of the break-up was partners and husbands leaving for other women. Almost half of these were due to partners working away from home. It would therefore appear that the emergence of an increasing number of single mothers is a direct result of urbanization and labour migration where men contract new liaisons in their new places of employment. For instance, Renting's husband went to work in Saratok and subsequently told her that he had contracted another marriage there. However, they are still legally married. Renting lost contact with him for five years and did not know his whereabouts. Khoo's husband found work in Batu Niah and took another wife there. Their divorce is pending. Jeema married her third partner, a fellow Bidayuh by native customary rights. After their child was born, he left to work in Kuala Lumpur and never returned for nine years. The last she heard of him was that he married an Indonesian woman and was now a Muslim. Norhani's abusive husband left to work in peninsular Malaysia and has not been heard of for the last five years. She now has to support four children on her wage of RM300 a month as a domestic worker.

Large extended families are double-edged swords. Although they provide much needed support, the stress and strain of familial relations are potential marriage breakers. After third-party involvement, financial insecurity and domestic violence, interference of family members was the fourth most commonly cited cause of marital fragmentation. The story of Tina below illustrates what happens when in-laws come into the picture.

Tina, an Iban, aged 26, was divorced from her husband and lived with a cousin in Kapit with her two sons, aged three and two. When she first married, she stayed with her parents-in-law as her husband was an only son. After the birth of her first child, she moved back to her own village and her husband followed. Her husband left her after the birth of the second child and moved back to his parents. This is what Tina said,

> My mother and father-in-law didn't like me. In addition, my father-in-law was mentally unstable. People in the longhouse said that my mother-in-law went to see the shaman to get my husband to dislike/hate me. My heart is heavy, my children are small and I don't know what to do. My mother is old, my father is no longer alive. Life is very difficult. [*Mak dan bapa mertua memang tidak suka saya. Tambah pula bapa mertua ada sakit jiwa. Orang sama rumah panjang cakap mak mertua ada jumpa manang suruh suami tidak suka/benci pada saya. Susah hati, anak masih kecil, tidak tahu apa nak buat. Mak sudah tua, bapa tak ada lagi. Cukup susah dan seksa.*]

Her mother told Tina to leave home and stay with her cousin in Kapit as they could not survive in the longhouse. Her long-suffering cousin was therefore landed with three additional dependents plus his own family. In spite of the fragmentation of marriages, the institution of family is still very strong in Sarawak. Often in our interviews we encountered families pulling together in difficult circumstances to help less fortunate members of their households.

Lucy's urban extended household also proved to be the undoing of her marriage. Lucy's husband earned RM350 a month as a storekeeper. He tried to get a factory job but quit after a short time as he had a heart condition and could not stand the hard work. They stayed with Lucy's parents and five of her siblings in a low-cost terrace house. Lucy's husband could not get along with the other family members and wanted to move out to a rented room. Lucy was reluctant as they could not be financially independent and her parents also objected. Finally, the stress and strain became too much and they divorced.

As these narratives show, causes of marital fragmentation are often multiple and complex — early age at first marriage; migration and employment mobility as a result of rapid urbanization; financial insecurity; and third-party interference, are all contributory factors. Our findings are therefore contrary to the view that marital breakdown is a consequence of a collapse in moral and family values. On the contrary, divorce and marital dissolution were not taken lightly and was resorted to only when all attempts at reconciliation failed. More than half of the respondents attempted to salvage the relationship by getting advice and help from family members, village elders and for the Muslims, the Islamic law courts [*mahkamah syari' a*] while the rest tried to locate the errant partner and persuade him to return. It must be pointed out again here that in rural villages, parents and village elders often step in to reconciliate couples. Migrants in urban centres frequently do not have elder kinsfolk to assist them in such matters and are left to flounder on their own. The lack of state support of single mothers and their low education meant that the majority of these women could not earn a living wage. Although they were trapped in unhappy marriages, they had no choice but to endure them and seek a reconciliation. Thus, for the majority of women, separation and divorce were the last resort. It is interesting that more urban than rural respondents attempted to save the relationship. This contradicts the expectation that village norms and censure would be more likely to keep married couples together in comparison to their urban sisters living in the anonymous urban environment. However, I believe that this is an outcome of the class position of the women who were interviewed. Urban single mothers from the lower socio-economic strata were more vulnerable than their rural counterparts as they had less supportive networks. Table 6.6 shows the number of respondents who attempted to save their relationships and their location.

TABLE 6.6
Number of Respondents who Attempted to Save Their Relationships, and Their Location

Location	Attempts made to save the relationship			Total
	Yes	No	No response	
Urban	61 (50%)	40 (33%)	21 (17%)	122 (100%)
Rural	46 (42%)	56 (51%)	7 (7%)	109 (100%)

Most of the respondents had very mixed feelings about the break-up of their relationships. It was a relief and a release for many to be rid of a tortuous relationship but, on the other hand, single motherhood brought with it a different set of problems, as we shall soon see in the next section.

4. Problems Faced

Women at different phases of their life-cycle reported different types of problems. Young single mothers (in the 21–30 years age bracket) suffered more emotionally and had the greatest childcare problems compared with older single mothers (those aged 41–50 years). It is not surprising that urban single mothers with a much diminished support network complained more about emotional and physical problems of shelter and problems with dependents when compared to their rural sisters in the villages. However, the latter have greater financial problems. Tija recounted the story of how she used to lock her young children in the house every time she went out to work. This nearly led to a tragedy when a fire broke out in the squatter area where they lived. Fortunately, the children were rescued in time. Tija's case aptly illustrates the problems of childcare and shelter for an urban single mother. Another urban single mother encountered in our interviews lived in a squatter settlement where her house stood in the midst of her neighbour's toilets.

Conclusion

This chapter has tried to show that labour mobility as a result of rapid urbanization has led to increasing fragmentation of families and marriages as men contract new liaisons and marriages in their new employment locations in urban centres. It also looked at the different experiences of rural and urban single mothers in the lower socio-economic strata and several points need reiteration. First, rural single mothers are more likely to have had an arranged marriage and be married by customary rites in the village when compared to their urban sisters. They are also more poorly educated and have fewer employment opportunities by virtue of their remote geographical location. As a result, more of them are unemployed but when they are employed, they work mainly in the agricultural sector, while their urban counterparts usually find employment in the service sector. Frequently, urban single mothers hold down multiple jobs and therefore suffer less from financial problems than their rural sisters.

However, rural single mothers have greater support networks from their kin in the villages. This perhaps explains why they do not try as hard as their urban counterparts to seek reconciliation with their partners.

Contrary to the common view held by the media and government officials that there is a breakdown in family values, the findings revealed that the family is alive and well in Sarawak. Grandparents, parents, siblings, cousins and other kin often rallied round and were the first line of support for single mothers. In other words, single motherhood did not necessarily lead to female headed households but was more likely to result in multi-generation extended households as single mothers moved in with their natal families once again. This leads to the debunking of yet another myth. It has been a worry of the authorities that children of single mothers are a potential source of social problems. This is premised on the belief that children brought up solely by their mothers have no masculine role models and authority for a strong identity. Consequently, this leads to involvement in illegal and undesirable activities in order to achieve alternative recognition. Needless to say, there are many counter arguments to such a commonly held belief in Malaysia. It suffices to say here that far from the stereotypical image of the urban nuclear family suffering from isolation and rootlessness, the resurrection of an extended household when a nuclear family fragments meant that child-rearing by conjugal tie is not the only model of parenting. Social parenting by siblings and others through kinship ties is equally important, and sometimes more important than conjugal parenting. Thus, the alienating forces of urbanization are attenuated by familial support networks in the context of the experiences of single mothers in Sarawak.

Notes

1. This chapter is part of a larger study, another aspect of which has been published in *SOJOURN* 18, no. 1 (April 2003).
2. The vulnerability of Muslim marriages has been well studied (see Tan and Jones 1990).
3. As principal researcher, I would like to acknowledge the other researchers on the team: Song Saw Imm and Rasidah Mahdi from Universiti Teknologi Mara (UiTM).
4. Single mothers in this study belong to the lower socio-economic strata.
5. Frequently, single women who migrate to the towns for employment, return to their natal villages during special occasions and celebrations like the

harvest festival [*gawai*] and Christmas. This is particularly so for the indigenous communities who are mainly Christians.

6. Pepper posts used for the climbing vines are made of *belian* which is a tropical hardwood. Each *belian* pepper post would cost approximately RM8.
7. Padawan is a rural area in the outskirts of Kuching.
8. *Tangkap basah* is the local Malay phrase for *khalwat* in Islam. Under *syari'a* law, if a man and a woman who are not legally related are caught in close proximity in an isolated place, the Muslim person involved will be charged in the Islamic court.

References

Berger, Brigitte and Peter Berger. "The War Over the Family". In *Marriage and Family in a Changing Society*, edited by Henslin, James. New York: Free Press, 1992.

Bilton, Tony, Kevin Bonnett, Philip Jones, Michelle Stanworth, Ken Sheard and Andrew Webster. *Introductory Sociology*. London: Macmillan Press, 1987.

Department of Statistics, Malaysia, 2000.

Jabatan Kemajuan Islam Malaysia.

Moore, Henrietta. *Is there a Crisis in the Family?* Occasional Paper no. 3, World Summit for Social Development, 1994.

Pearson, Ruth. "Gender Issues in Industrialization". In *Industrialization and Development*, edited by Hewitt, Tom, Hazel Johnson, Dave Wield. Oxford: Oxford University Press, 1994.

Tan Poo Chang and Gavin Jones. "Malay Divorce in Peninsular Malaysia: The Near-disappearance of an Institution", *Southeast Asian Journal of Social Science* 18, no. 2 (1990): 85–114.

Secombe, Wally. *Weathering the Storm: Working-class Families from the Industrial Revolution to the Fertility Decline*. U.K. and U.S.A: Verso, 1993.

7

From Highlands to Lowlands
Kelabit Women and Their Migrant Daughters

Poline Bala

Introduction: The Highlands, Kelabit and Isolation

A survey conducted in 1998 revealed that 63.8 per cent of the total Kelabit population have migrated out of the highlands (Murang 1998).[1] This is highly significant for the Kelabit people who forty years ago were considered remote and unreachable. Harrisson,[2] one of the first white writers to arrive in the area described it as one of the "...few [places] where, in fact, you cannot be more away from what most people call 'the world'. There are fewer places where you (or I) are likely to be able to feel more remote, more 'cut off' from the great outside..." (Harrisson 1959, p. 5). As a result, lowlanders like the people of Tinjar area have always considered the Kelabit to be living in "another world" fabled for its "big men, sexy women, cold nights, rich harvests, irrigation, inaccessibility, cattle and goats" (Harrisson 1959, p. 152). Not many understood their way of life and in fact, at the turn of the twentieth century, were deemed "lost", "terrible, troublesome and apathetic drunkards", and "on the way out" (Hudson 1999; Crain and Pearson-Rounds 1999).

Why is this so? The Kelabit Highland is a highland plateau with an average altitude of approximately 1,000 metres above sea level. It is located above the furthest reaches of the navigable rivers of Baram and Limbang in the north-east of Sarawak. It is surrounded by rugged mountains, high peaks and dense jungle. In order to reach the area, one had to wade through dense forest, climb high peaks, negotiate rugged mountains, go through deep valleys, manoeuvre the crossing and recrossing of ranges and streams. Therefore the Kelabit Highland is considered by those who are unfamiliar with the area to be unfriendly and dangerous.

This chapter gives an overview of Kelabit rural-urban migration in Sarawak and considers how Kelabit women experience migration and their responses to it. It examines issues confronting the women left behind and those who have left their homeland, through the art form of stories and songs. It uses *lakuh* — an oral tradition used by women in the highlands to narrate some of their experiences of urbanization and rural-urban migration. This is a theme of which the author is familiar, as a Kelabit woman who was born and raised in the highlands and who inevitably joined the flow of migrants down to the lowlands of Sarawak. Thus, the voices of my informants will be joined by my own personal narrative.

Kelabit Rural-urban Migration: Cause and Consequence

Growing up in the highlands, the rugged terrain formed a fortress of refuge defining the boundaries of my world. Mountains, valleys and streams made up the landscape where my dreams were germinated and my curiosity nurtured. Unlike my ancestors who have ventured into the outside world, I had never crossed those mountains as a child — Mount Murud to the north, Tamabuh Range to the west and Uwat Range to the east. My only access to the world beyond those mountains was through personal narratives in the form of songs and stories by members of our community who had taken long journeys to conduct barter trade with other groups downriver. Their stories of these far away places stirred a curiosity and desire to explore the world outside the highlands.

In spite of its geographical isolation, historically there were in fact many links between the Kelabit world and in Harrison's words, "the great outside" world (1959, p. 5). There have been connections and networks between the Kelabit and other ethnic groups in Borneo for generations. In fact, one of the defining characteristics of the people of Borneo is their high level of geographical mobility. For instance, the Kelabit had barter trade links with the Kayan, Kenyah, Berian, Potok, Kerayan, Murut downriver and also with the Chinese and Malay along the coast.

For me growing up in the highlands, these links with the world outside was substantiated through the presence of many non-locally produced material objects such as old dragon jars [*belanai ma'un*], beads [*ba'o*], machetes [*tungul*] and Chinese jugs [*angai*] in the longhouses. Many of these objects were obtained from the "great outside" for everyday use in the highlands. Once these objects reached the longhouses, they were adapted into the Kelabit way of life. One clear example is the appropriation of T'ang and Ming Chinese jars into the Kelabit stratification system. They were more than just storage jars for rice wine [*burak*] used in ceremonies. These jars, especially the old dragon jars, were considered prestige items and status symbols for members of the aristocratic strata in Kelabit society[3] (Saging 1979; Talla 1979; Janowski 1991). Many of these valuable objects were acquired from other traders in exchange for tobacco, salt, rice, *gutta percha* and resin from the highlands. These dynamic relations of exchange crossed cultural and ethnic lines and were very important not only for the Kelabit but also for the various groups in the interior including the Dayaks and the Malays (Rousseau 1989).

The meaning and the value of these prestige items in the Kelabit longhouses must be understood within the context of their difficult journeys in bringing them to the highlands. Prior to the introduction of air transportation into the highlands in the 1950s, it took the Kelabit at least three to four weeks on a one-way journey on foot or by boat to transport these valuables into the highlands. It is the hardship endured on such journeys [*me ngerang*] that provided meanings and prestige to these items.[4]

Nowadays, of course, it is the pursuit of education and not barter trade and objects of desire which is the main catalyst for the outward migration from the highlands (Murang 1998). The introduction of formal education marked an important watershed in the history of the Kelabit people who were illiterate before 1946. In fact, the first recorded outward migration of Kelabit for education was in the year 1958 (Lee and Bahrin 1993). Today, the literacy rate amongst the Kelabit, particularly amongst the younger generations, is high. Many have at least a secondary school leaving certificate (after eleven years of formal schooling), while others have local and foreign university degrees. Still others have attended professional courses and are working as civil servants and in the private sector across the country. In other words, the Kelabit have been very successful in their quest for formal education in spite of numerous difficulties. It is not uncommon for the pioneering students to walk five to seven days through thick rainforest to get to the nearest school and many had to leave home at a tender age of six or seven to attend boarding school outside their villages. Such hardships meant that those who succeeded would have to migrate to urban areas in order to find work which is on par with their educational achievements. Over the years, the Kelabit Highlands have been emptied of its sons and daughters.

According to a survey conducted by Lee and Bahrin (1993) on ninety-three households in the highlands, each household had at least one person who had migrated or moved away. They found that "about one third had at least two members who had migrated; one third had at least three-four members; and another one third had between five and ten migrants from their household (ibid., p. 118). In other words, almost every family in the highlands is involved in the migration process. Amster (1998) argued that large scale population movement has coloured Kelabit social landscape today. In fact out of a population of 5,002 Kelabit in the year 2000,[5] only 1,500 remain in the highlands while others have moved away for further education and better job opportunities in urban areas such as Miri, Kuching, Sibu, Bintulu, Kuala Lumpur and even overseas.

In my own family, none of my seven other siblings live permanently in the highlands. My own migration trajectory is an illustration of the significance of formal education as a motivating force for leaving. I left at the age of fourteen after completing my third year in secondary school. The two secondary schools in the highlands did not offer classes beyond the third year. I continued my secondary education in Miri which is an hour's flight from the Kelabit Highlands. I moved again when I enrolled in a university in Kuala Lumpur. Five years later, I returned to live in Sarawak, this time in Kuching.

However, a year later, I left to pursue a Masters degree in Ithaca, New York, USA. On completion of my course, I returned to Kuching. Two years later in 2003, I left yet again to pursue my Ph.D. in Cambridge, UK.

This massive population movement has led to a major shift in our history as a people from being an isolated and self-sufficient group[6] to a global diaspora. Many Kelabit have since ventured into various careers, which are completely different from our traditional ones. In the past forty years, the Kelabit have responded and adapted themselves to changes in politics, economics, education, culture and technology which has transformed them from a rice-farming oriented community to one that produces professionals, religious leaders and intellectuals who play important roles in the wider Malaysian society. In this way, the previously invisible inhabitants of the Kelabit Highlands have now entered mainstream Malaysian life.

Narratives [*sekunuh*] of Those Left Behind

When I asked for stories about their journeys into the faraway land downriver, some of these grandparents [*tepu*], mothers and aunts [*sina*], fathers and uncles [*tama*] would narrate their stories while others would sing them out to me. I remember how as a child these stories and songs would trigger curiosity about the world outside my own village. Why stories and songs? Like many other oral communities, the Kelabit traditionally passed down their experiences through art, story-telling and songs. These songs are songs of personal experience [*lakuh*], songs describing the exploits of heroes and heroines long ago [*benging*] and long narratives of warrior epics [*sedadai/sedarir*] (Bala 2002).

Although a dying custom amongst the Kelabit, some of these traditional songs are still recited by the older generation in the longhouses. The *lakuh*, for example, are still being composed and sung by women in the villages. *Lakuh,* like other traditional Kelabit songs are narration of personal experiences except that these songs are composed mainly by women in the community. Unlike other songs, Rubenstein (1991, p. 140), suggests that a *lakuh* is used to "describe completely a person's state of being at a particular time of crisis", and that they are usually "intensely personal and generally definitive as a result of being developed over a period of time".

When the women in the highlands were asked to talk about their experiences with migration, the most common complaint was that it was "too quiet" or "lonely" [*da'at ali*] as so many young people were away in town. Many said that they miss their children very much. In fact, one woman confided, "Had I known that my children would leave me and my husband, I would have forbidden them to go to school. I think of them while in the farm, while sitting by the fireplace, while collecting vegetables. The house is very empty without them." This loneliness is lamented through songs, particularly the *lakuh*. I have collected a number of *lakuh* by various women over the years but for the purpose of this chapter, I wish to highlight two *lakuh*. The first one is by Ngelinuh Karuh and the second is by Doo Ilah.

Ngelinuh Karuh is in her eighties and lives in Bario Asal with her husband Pun Besara. She has eight children and twenty-three grandchildren. None of her children [*anak*] and grandchildren [*mupun*] live with them in the longhouse. She complains of loneliness as all her children have left the highlands to live in cities and towns. Her *lakuh* goes like this:

This thunder clangs [*Legku sinih turun*]

Silently, nicely I sit in the kitchen [*Pirud doo tudo tuih lem takep*]

Putting on my lap, Toni a good child [*Neh ngabin Toni, anak doo atek*]

A child given by God to be happy with [*Anak bire Tuan inan liat-liat*]

Slowly, I stand up without a sound [*Ngae the uih neh mudur na' am mawan raseb*]

Opening the door for the sun to appear [*Neh ngukap bubpu' dalan edto mirat*]

I look downriver over the flat lands [*Mupo me la' ud uih lem tana' belad*]

In the fertile land where the *udat* grows well [*Lem tana' baling kelunan udat*]

Where rice grows evenly at the same height [*Kelunan pade udung rumpaad*]

A place trodden by people from times past [*Bawang kelayan dulun let ngilad*]

A place visited by visitors from all over the place [*Bawang pitan sakai pelamud irat*]

Suddenly in my soul I search [*Ulit neh lem burur kuh neh tekap-tekap*]

Tears from the eyes drop with a drip [*Mirat ebpa mateh tutu' neh tehpek*]

Tears drop onto the sarong [*Ebpa mateh tutu' me luun lekab*]

Onto the *sarong tajung pelikat*[7] [*Luun kelibung tajung pelikat*]

My mind wanders thinking of my children [*Tekap me selinuh kuh ngarawe anak*]

Thinking of Temabu and his siblings [*Ngelinuh Temabu ideh dinganak*]

They have all moved over the mountain range [*Nange neh ideh buro la mibal apad*]

Left to live in a difficult place [*Buro me mulun lem bawang mikat*]

Living in a place with no sibling [*Mulun lem bawang na' am kinanak*]

Without a mother to comfort them [*Na' am teh tesinah inan palap iat*]

Remembering our time in the past [*Kesikanan ayu kedi tauh ngilad*]

The time when we farmed downriver [*Ridtu me lam lati' pela' ud natad*]

We went to pull the weeds that were overgrown [*Me ngerabut uduh nuk pelaba mapet*]

Weeds in the slippery soil very difficult to pull [*Uduh luan liyu' pelaba mikat*]

And that is why I am sad [*Inih men nuk inan kuh da' at iat*]

Cannot bear the thought of difficult tasks [*Na' am ke the linuh ngen edten mikat*]

No one to ask to go back and cook [*Na'am the nuk ru'en narih muli me ngelaak*]

To ask to collect pumpkin leaves [*Ru'en narih me merin edtah da'un tedtak*]

To collect leaves in the fertile land with *desat* [*Me ngalap da'un lem baling desat*]

To collect wood for cooking [*Me ngalap kayuh tu'en pengelaak*]

Suddenly this thunder rolls [*Ulit men legku sinih tuna-tuna*]

Thundering slowly towards the dawn [*Legku ai ai me matun rami'a*]

Getting up early to pray in the morning [*Tui lekadtang uih sembayang muka*]

Asking Father the Big Man Lord God [*Neh mutuh Tama La'ih Tuan Allah*]

Asking Him to help in the big things [*Mutuh lah nulung narih ngen nuk rayeh-rayeh*]

Until all the children can open their eyes [*Medting ngen anak narih bulat matah*]

To include the few grandchildren I have [*Medting ngen mupun narih nuk duah*]

To make us wise to obey His words [*Naru' kamih milah maya' karuh lah*]

Going to heaven a big place [*Me bawang surga lem tana' rayeh*]

Where we sing praising Lord God [*Inan tauh menani ngubur Tuan Allah*]

Praising Lord Jesus and the Father [*Ngubur Tuan Isut diweh dengetameh*]

Putting the water in the pot with one handle [*Neh nebpa' lajang ka'ul nuk midteh*]

My mind wandered about having no rice [*Tekap selinuh kuh neh na'am bera*]

There's no child to ask to pound [*Na'am men anak tu'en me tupeh*]

That's when tears come out of my eyes [*Ineh men pu'un kuh mirat ebpa mateh*]

Tears from my eyes dripping onto my sarong [*Ebpa mateh tutu luun ta'a*]

Onto the sarong with intricate designs [*Luun kelibung barit pelima*]

When the sun disappears [*Idih beto'edto tanep temapa*]

That's when I begin to be troubled [*Ineh neh ouun kuh pelaba tuseh*]

Thinking about us, mother and children [*Kesikanen ayu tauh dengesinah*]

When we went working in the big wet rice fields [*Ridtu' me lema'ud lem baa rayeh*]

To pull the very overgrown weeds [*Me ngerabut uduh mapet pelaba*]

Weeds constantly growing on slippery ground [*Uduh luan liyu mulun tuna-tuna*]

Those are the things that haunt me [*Inih neh nuk inan kuh da' at awa*]

It saddened me having to work hard [*Da' at men iat kuh rupu' temuna*]

There is no one to ask to go back early [*Na' am the lun ru' en muli'mageh*]

To make rice in the single pot [*Me naru' nuba' lem lajang edtah*]

To collect leaves for the wrappings[8] [*Me ngalap da' un inan narih nenga*]

To collect wood in the deep jungle [*Me ngalap kayuh lem pulung kura*]

In case my words will be shortened [*Tulu men narih bebpi' binala*]

When I go Home with open eyes [*Renga narih me muli bulat lem mateh*]

What a pity that my grandchildren will suffer [*Mai the ada' mupun narih la' pederah*]

Looking after what I have left at that time [*La' nu' uh a' un narih kereb ridtu' ineh*]

If only I have faith in Him [*Tulu teden uih menu Ngeneh*]

I will rise alone and they will not be troubled [*Mudur sebulen na' am the ideh tuseh*]

I will ascend up and they will not suffer [*Mudur uir telupu na' am teh ideh dereh*]

This is the end of my *lakuh*, the thunder rolls on [*Inih neh paad lakuh kuh legku tuna-tuna*]

In case somebody remembers to say [*Awe' edtah burur la kesikenan mala*]

"Why is she saying this *lakuh*?" [*Mala lakuh kudeh iah doo tuna-tuna*]

It's a *lakuh* said with tears from my eyes [*Lakuh nuk binala kuh mirat ebpa mateh*]

Thinking of children who moved and left [*Nengelinuh anak nuk neh buro nedteh*]

Hornbill, this is my *lakuh* [*Menidun dih lakuh*]

The next *lakuh* is composed by Doo Ilah who is originally from Pa Lungan, but now lives in Bario Asal with her husband. She lives next door to Ngelinuh Karuh. Unlike Ngelinuh Karuh, Doo Ilah has two sons living in Bario[9] — Balan Paran (Lawai) and Paran Matu (Peter). However, all her other seven children have migrated to different parts of the country: Sina Ngegkang Ulun (Muda) in Marudi; Sina Galih Balang (Ubong) in Sibu; Sinah Ngimet Aren (Sigang) in Miri; Balang Belaan (Kenneth), Sinah Paran Lem Uned (Dayang) and Temabu Alan Matu in Kuching; and Noel in Kuala Lumpur.

Like her neighbour's *lakuh*, Doo Ilah's theme is loneliness and the
sadness she felt when her eldest daughter (Sina Ngegkang Ulun @ Muda)
married and left home to settle in Marudi with her husband Wan Malang,
a Berawan young man. When asked how she felt when her daughter left.
She replied, "I felt so alone at that time." She had never experienced
loneliness before. This was even when her father, Udan Turun, died when
she was young. She was brought up by her uncle, Aren Tuan (see line 22).
In conversation, Doo Ilah talked about the joy, comfort and security she
enjoyed whilst staying with her uncle.

The thunder rolls on [*Legku sinih turun*]
Quietly let us sit squatting [*Pirud doo tudo tauh tekukung*]
Sitting in the home of Melayung Ulun [*Tudo lem rumah Melayung Ulun*]
Sitting side by side with the old large jars [*Tudo neh pelalad ngen belanai
    maun*]
The jars that belonged to my father [*Belanai tama' meto' lat puun*]
Slowly I got up [*Ayan teh uih neh mudur ulit ame layun*]
Standing under the open roof with the *belaung*[10] support [*Mudur liang
    ikab tukul belaung*]
My thoughts wander as I am all alone [*Tekap selinuh kuh naam lun
    ruyung*]
Thoughts of my Senamu', my eldest child [*Ngelinuh Senamu' uih suk anak
    puun*]
They are living in places by a river mouth [*Nange kedidah mulun lem
    bawang elung*]

Living in Marudi, an ancient place [*Mudeng Marudi suk bawang pu'un*]
Including Noel, my youngest child [*Medting kuh Noel suk anak udung*]
Together with Temamu, Ngegkang Ulun [*Peruyung ngan tememu' laih
    Ngegkang Ulun*]
In case someone remembers to ask [*Awe' edtah burur ela' sekenan ngitun*]
Why are you singing your *lakuh*? [*Mala lakuh ngudeh iko doo turun-
    turun*]
Remembering Aken[11] in another distant place [*Ngelinuh Aken uih lem
    bawang elung*]
Living in Kuching that far away place [*Lem bawang Kuching lem bawang
    elung*]
Dayang is there with them [*Medting kuh Dayang nange teh iyeh ruyung*]

Together with Tememu' Balang Ngelibun[12] [*Peruyung ngen Tememu'*
   Balang Ngelibun]
My own thoughts wander [*Tekap neh selinuh neh keduih*]
No children living together with me [*Naam teh anak inan kuh peruyung*]
Living together with uncle Aren Tuan [*Peruyung ngen tama' Aren Tuan*]
Slowly I got up [*Ayan teh uih neh mudur*]
Went to the fertile farm with *ubong* [*Mine uih lem latih baling ubong*]

Working among the maize laden with fruits [*Lati' lem dele buah peluun*]
Under the abundant ears of rice [*Lati' lem pade keruyob udung*]
Praising the Lord God who gives me life [*Ngubur Tuhan Allah uih nuk neh*
   ngulun]
He gives me life, dear hornbill, this is my song [*Ngulun kuh Manidun, dih*
   lakuh]

The experiences of Ngelinuh Karuh and Doo Ilah resonate with Sinah
Tidan's experience from Pa Ramapuh. The laments of these women
encapsulate the unspoken experiencs of many women, mainly mothers as
their children leave for the urban areas. Like many others in the highlands,
Sinah Tidan married at the tender age of fifteen. She is now a widow with
seven children. She lives in a big longhouse constantly pining for her
children who have migrated to the lowlands. Her children take turns to
return to the highlands at least once a year. Her late husband once said,
"She wants all her children to come back and there are a lot tears when
they leave." Another mother lamented, "Education and marriage have
taken our children away from Bario. When they do come back it is only for
a short while."

Narratives of Those who Left

And what of these women's daughters in cities? This is what is considered
in this section. Do these daughters also suffer loneliness and sadness like
their mothers in the highlands? Do they lament the loss of the comfort of
home? Why did they leave in the first place? Was it difficult for them to
discard their rural lifestyle in exchange for an urban way of life?

   The stories of Sarah, Rebekah, Rachel and Ruth give us a glimpse of
the experiences of women migrants to the lowlands.

   Sarah was one of the first Kelabit women to go to school and left her village in Long Lellang to study in Long Moh until Primary Four. When asked why she went to school, she said that initially, she was reluctant to go to school but her father spanked her and told her "I regard you like a son. You must complete your study until you become a teacher. Only then can you get married." [*Paad ni' er anak dela' ih teh uih ngemuh. Mesti mengah sekulah mudih medting iko kuh guru. Let nginah neh iko ngaweh*]."

Eventually she enjoyed school because it was new and different. She had an innate curiosity and a desire to learn how to read and write. On completion of Primary Four in Long Moh, Sarah was selected to continue her studies at St. Columbus School in Miri. However, there were no dormitories for girls at that school and she ended up at the Community Development School with Tuan Sapu[13] in Long Lamah. It was in Long Lamah while in Primary Five that she married her husband. How did that happen, I asked her. Sarah recounted her story. Her husband, Amir went to meet Tuan Sapu about his intention. Arrangement was made to seek permission from Sarah's father. To her amazement, her father agreed to the marriage proposal.

After her marriage, she and her husband returned to live in Bario as her husband was appointed an agricultural officer. Two years later, the family moved to Pa Main, her husband's village. In 1964 they moved back to Long Lamah where their first child, Agnes was born. In 1965, her husband entered party politics. The following year, he became a member of the district council and the family returned to Bario. But when her children had to leave Bario for further studies, they relocated outside Bario to be closer to them as well as to secure a stable income to support the children through school. When I asked how, she responded:

> We left Bario with nothing and went to Long Temala. There we started a small canteen but after a few years, your uncle decided to move to Marudi. While in Marudi, we bought and sold *kayuh garu*[14] from the Penan.[15] For a while, we dwelled amongst the Penan. After that, we started a pig farm in Marudi. Our next move was to Kuching. He took Gerald[16] and I to Kuching where he started a company selling encyclopedia and books. The business became the basis of our livelihood in Kuching. However, it was also the beginning of his illness. He died a few years later. I moved back to Marudi and have been in Marudi ever since.

Sarah believed strongly in education. She added, "Education is very important. It helped me to cope with living outside the village. Therefore,

I was very keen to put my children through school [*nu'uh anak sekulah*]. Education is a means to move up in society and to have access to better jobs and a more comfortable life." She ended the interview with this advice, "Education is like a walking stick used to prop up one's body [*kuh rukud peh ngiuk burur narih*]."

Another migrant from the village of Pa Umur expressed a similar notion regarding education. Rebekah began her education at Bario Primary School and then went on to Bario Secondary School from 1971 to 1973. She later moved to Marudi to pursue Form Four and Form Five. She completed her secondary school education in Miri in 1977. She continued her studies at a teachers' training college in Kuching and graduated two years later. In the last twenty-five years, Rebekah has taught in different places. She was in Marudi, Long Panai and Miri, moving every five to six years. When asked whether she had ever dreamt of leaving Bario when she was a child, Rebekah replied:

> Yes! When I was a student, I had to work hard in the farm in order to pay my school fees. It was four *gantang*[17] of rice a month, which was a lot especially in those days. It was a heavy burden if you come from a big family. Can you imagine the amount of work involved when a family has four children to send to school at the same time? That would be about sixteen *gantangs* of rice every month. Besides, one has to pound (*tupah*) the rice since there was no rice mill in those days. We also had to carry the rice on our backs (*mabeh*) to the school. One of my teachers used to say, 'If you don't study hard, baskets will be strapped onto your forehead for the rest of your life.' Therefore, I made a commitment that I will not be a farmer. However, my parents did not have the money for me to continue schooling. I wanted to quit and work as a maid but one of my teachers, Mr. Tan was very kind and helped pay my school fees. He told my father that I was an above average student. Seeing other Kelabits who made it to Marudi or Miri for studies also motivated me to persevere in my studies.

Another migrant daughter, Rachel left Bario for Miri after Primary Six. Unlike Rebekah who longed to further her education, Rachel was forced out of the highlands for "her own good". This is her story:

> I was forced to leave Bario because my parents really wanted me to further my studies. I didn't do well in primary school because my family was always on the move. We were in Long Balong, Bario, Pa Main and frequently moved between Arur Telal and Ulung Palang.[18] I refused to be

sent away to school. My parents had to persuade me. I cried so much because I was asked to leave. If it wasn't for Uncle Jack and family in Miri, I wouldn't have left Bario.

She continued:

I remember having to walk to school with other kids who were not Kelabit. It was quite an experience to be surrounded by so many non-Kelabit. It was tough trying to befriend them. I was only in Form One. I remember crying for my parents especially in the evenings. I returned to Bario in 1973 but a year later, I was asked to go to school in Kuching. After finishing secondary school in Kuching, I learnt typing. I worked for a timber company afterwards and a-year-and-a-half later, I got married. I was 22 years old then, which was considered quite old for a woman in those days. I have been following my husband ever since.

Anne now lives in Miri and has three teenage children.

Unlike Sarah, Rebekah and Rachel who left the highlands because of education, Ruth left because of marriage. She did not follow in the footsteps of the others in going to the lowlands but migrated cross the border to Kalimantan and to a different country. Ruth, a 38-year-old who has now returned to live in Bario again has this to tell:

At 14 years old, I was asked to stop studying in order to marry Temamu'. I was very, very reluctant and cried my heart out the night I was told, but the decision was already made for me. Temamu' was in Arur Dalan and my grandfather promised him a bride. Actually, the arrangement was for my cousin to marry him but that fell through. So, I had to bear the brunt of it. My grandfather said that he was unable to look after us. I left Bario for Kalimantan crying all the way. I had no clue what the future had in store for me. My husband and I went to live in Tarakan. I met many different groups of people and learnt to speak Javanese and Bugis. We ran a small business selling foodstuff. We returned to Bario in 1998 when times were bad. As my children are going to school here, I will live here to be close to them.

From the narratives of these women, education and marriage appear to be the two most significant reasons for women leaving the highlands. While some were eager to leave, others were reluctant and compelled to leave. Inspite of such differences, almost everyone spoke of the difficulties of adapting to an urban lifestyle. Rebekah commented:

As I see it, the main difference between life in Bario and life in town is that in Bario, we live in a community where we know almost everyone quite well. We know people by their names, who their parents and relatives are. It is so different in town, where you don't even know your own neighbours. I really miss community living. I long to be with our people — our own people and community. I miss the slow life in Bario where it is quiet and serene. It is very noisy here in town. In Miri, one is always rushing to school, to pay bills and so on. It is a hectic life.

I asked her if she would ever return to live in Bario. "Yes, I have a constant longing for Bario and dream of retiring there. I would really like to have my own flower garden and vegetable garden there. Right now, I have to live in Miri because I work here and I'm married to a non-Kelabit. All these things keep me from going home to Bario."

For Rachel, living with one's relatives [*lun ruyung*] was a real boon. She said:

> It made a lot of difference. I think if I hadn't stay with my relatives, I don't think I would have coped in town on my own. I wasn't happy leaving Bario at all, but thankfully, I had relatives to help me. They taught me how to cross the road, how to sit in a car, how to buy things in shops. In fact, they were the ones who encouraged me to get married as well! They also asked me to go to church. Most Kelabits go to church on Sundays, so you meet them in the service. It makes you feel that you are not alone at all. I hardly saw my parents. It was very difficult for them to come down to meet me. I would go home to Bario once a year and my father would come to visit me once a year. Sometimes my mom didn't come down for more than a year.

There is a major contrast between living in the rural areas and the urban areas. Lee and Bahrin suggested that the education process begun in the highlands is one of the most important factors in alienating the Kelabit from a rural way of life. Most Kelabit in the highlands are subsistence rice farmers. Their permanent wet rice cultivation distinguishes them from the other natives in Sarawak, except for the Lun Bawang. They cultivate Bario rice, which is well known for its aroma, fine grains and pleasant taste. Besides cultivating rice, they also grow citrus fruits for domestic consumption. In the highlands, communal longhouses are still the basis of organizing social and political life although increasingly there is a tendency to build single houses scattered around in the villages. Such a lifestyle is a far cry from the middle-class lifestyle of the urban Kelabit professionals.

As Amster argues, the "practicalities of widespread urban migration and intermarriage in town define the contemporary Kelabit social landscape" (1998, p. 61). These processes have resulted in changes in Kelabit lifestyle and social relations in urban areas. In the highlands, daily life and social interaction are primarily governed by village values and communal activities. However, this is absent in the urban areas. In the urban areas, the Kelabit community is fragmented (Amster 1998). Hence, urban Kelabit have to create new ways to communicate and interact with one another. One of these ways is the formation of Kelabit associations in the urban areas where they can meet.

The next song [*sedarir*] was sung by Lillian Bulan during a Highlanders Games Carnival dinner organized by the Association of Kelabit based in Kuala Lumpur. It expressed a common feeling amongst many Kelabit women who now reside in the urban centres. Like the narrative of Rebekah earlier, it is a song of the constant longing for the highlands. It must be pointed out at this juncture that there has been a revival of interests in traditional songs amongst urban Kelabit. *Sedarir* in modern terms is a form of "rap" where someone takes the lead rhythmically, line by line, as the rest of the group echoes. Traditionally, they are epic songs composed and sung by men to describe their exploration and expeditions into the world outside the highlands. What is interesting to note here is that although the composer of this song is a woman, the intent of the song remains that of a *sedarir*, that is, it reflects an engagement with the world outside the highlands.

"Honorable people, may we have your attention, please [*Pirud kuh ligegka tauh keh lun buren*]
Here we are, children from across the seas [*Inih edting kamih anak dipar bawang*]
We deliberately flew in [*Maya' bilun kamih temengen marih*]
To meet with you, our uncles [*Marih papu' ngen tetamah menaken*]
And relatives we have longed to see [*Papu lun ruyung pelaba doo diren*]

We are from a magnificent place [*Kamih mirat let ngih bawang doo siren*]
A huge city with towering skylines [*Bawang rayeh ruma'dita' tungen-tungen*]
Indeed so beautiful and grand is the place we now live in [*Tu'ud doo bawang inan kamih mudeng*]
But nothing could take the place [*Na'am teh linuh narih la' peketeng*]

Of our own homeland upcountry in our hearts [*Ngelinuh lem bawang tauh lem puneng*]
That land where our forefathers lived [*Inan tetepuh tauh mudeng*]
Where they toiled [*Inan kedideh neh ngalap bareng*]
And gathered their wealth [*Ngineh teh inan deh neh ngalap bareng*]

Though the land is far and remote, where the night falls all too soon [*Tu'uh peh mado, edto saget mabi*]
Their homes are filled with fun [*Pelaba teh ramai nuk inan mudeng*]
Even in homes lit with resin lamps [*Pelaba teh medtang deh ngen ilu' nateng*]
The light of the moon and stars is theirs to leisurely behold [*Tudo liang edtang bulan dih gitu'en*]
They move about freely and fear nothing [*Nalan kukud na'am teh nuk metedteng*]
Their nights are calm and without distractions [*Rudap dedtem, na'am teh nuk megueng*]

What a contrast it is compared to the place we now live in [*Pelaba beken men lem inan kamih mudeng*]
The streets and highways are lighted all night long [*Lapung ngi dalan mulun kedangan*]
The rumbling sound of cars is there to stay [*Unih kereta dih pedingeren*]
People work from dawn till midnight [*Kereja mirat edto medting tangal alem*]
It is a "no money, no talk" business world [*Na'am usin, na'am ayu teh nuk kenen*]
Because there is no such thing as "free lunch" [*Na'am men nuk rinen narih lem muneng*]
It is "no car, no feet" daily ordeal [*Na'am kerita, na'am mired temen*]
Because it is just not practical nor safe to travel without wheels [*Na'am men nuk inan uleng-uleng*]

Indeed, nothing compares to our ancestral homeland upcountry [*Doo ayu bawang tetepuh lem puneng*]
No matter how broke one could be [*Na'am peh usin narih lem ragem*]
There are always, the wild vegetables to gather [*Inan teh kerid nuk kereb rinen*]

And wild animals to hunt [*Inan teh puung nuk kereb apen*]
For such things, one need not even spend a cent [*Bareng keminah na'am peh idih belien*]
They are always there for the taking! [*Medting tidih marih lem taneken*]

There are not enough reasons for our yearning [*Ineh neh nuk inan narih gelitemen*]
The reason for our constant longing [*Nuk na'am ketuh meleg lem linuen*]
For our ancestral homeland, the place we will return to [*Bawang tetepuh tu'en ngerineng*]

This is now from us [*Paad inih nuk kereb belaan*]
Who came across the seas [*Kamih nuk mirat let dipar bawang*]
We bring greetings from [*Marih muit tabi'*]
The Association of the Kelabits of Kuala Lumpur, Selangor [*Persatuan Kaum Kelabit Kuala Lumpur, Selangor*]

Conclusion

For the past forty years, the Kelabit have experienced major changes in their lives and history as a people. Outward migration undoubtedly is one of the most significant factors which has transformed the Kelabit from a rice-farming community to one that produces professionals, religious leaders, intellectuals and others who play a valuable role in wider Malaysian society. As suggested by the songs and narratives of women and their migrant daughters, these transformations are not without cost. Kelabit women, both rural and urban, pay a high price especially in terms of a loss of mutual support in mother-and-daughter relationships — mothers who have no daughters to help in the fields and hearth in the highlands and daughters in the city who have no maternal support as they engage in a modern, urban lifestyle. A vacuum is created and the yearning for each other is acute. These women turn to songs, their religion, education and urban kin to sustain them through such transformative times.

Notes

1. Unfortunately, the survey did not take into account gender as one of the important variables to consider. The survey is based on age, reasons for migration, level of education, occupation and ownership of houses in urban areas.

2. Tom Harrisson, FRGS, arrived in the highlands of Sarawak on the morning of 25 March 1945. With three others he parachuted from a RAF Liberator and landed in the Plain of Bah, commonly known today as Bario. The inhabitants of the area, today known as the Kelabit, joined Harrisson to fight the occupying Japanese Army. Eventually the Kelabit let Harrisson stay in their longhouses for much of his time during the war, and allowed him to return afterwards to stay for long periods among them as a friend. Harrisson subsequently had a Kelabit wife. Many years later, Harrisson chronicled some of his experiences living with the Kelabit in his classic book *"World Within: A Borneo Story"*.

3. Among the Kelabit until recently, only certain families owned these jars. They are prized as family heirlooms, particularly the 70-kilogram ceramic jar with the red dragon. Chin (1980) made similar observations on the value of beads. He writes, "… beads are highly mobile objects and have been traded into the hinterland of Borneo. Like ceramic and brass objects, beads form part of the traditional symbols of social status and wealth amongst the indigenous people. They are heirlooms handed down from one generation to the next, from mother to daughter. In the old days, beads were one of the principle forms of currency. Beads are also used as bride wealth and serve as grave goods among the aristocrats (1980, p. 49)."

4. For instance, one *belanai ma' un* was said to be worth a human life. Not only did a person have to travel many kilometres in months to obtain a *belanai ma' un*, but he also had to have enough wealth to exchange for one. For instance, it is suggested that a person had to have at least five buffaloes, five fat pigs, three humpback bulls, two goats, two ordinary jars, two gongs, two fine parang knives, ten mats, ten fish nets, ten fowls, ten Pa Mada pots, ten rolls of best leaf tobacco, one hundred yellow cane beads and two hundred packages of salt, to give in exchange for one *belanai ma' un*. It is therefore a sign of high status in the community to own a *belanai ma' un*.

5. The Kelabit are one of the smallest ethnic groups in Sarawak. Like other indigenous communities in rural Sarawak, the Kelabit traditionally live in communal longhouses although there has been a recent tendency to build single houses scattered around in the villages.

6. The Kelabit at one point was a self sufficient group — growing their own rice, producing salt from a couple of salt springs found in their homeland, and hunting and gathering jungle produce for a living.

7. A weaved sarong.

8. Packed lunch is taken to the farm and the food is wrapped in large leaves.

9. Bario is the largest village in the Kelabit Highlands.

10. *Belaung* is a type of local wood used to prop open a section of the roof.

11. Kenneth

12. Tememu' Balang Ngelibun is related to Doo Ilah and is currently the State Director of Immigration.

13. He was a Christian missionary by the name of Hudson Southwell.

14. A type of scented wood.
15. A semi nomadic forest group.
16. Her son.
17. One *gantang* is equivalent to 3.5 kilograms. A kilogram of rice costs RM5 or US$1.30.
18. Place names in the Kelabit Highlands.

References

Amster, M. H. *Community, Ethnicity, and Modes of Association among the Kelabit of Sarawak, East Malaysia.* Unpublished Ph.D. dissertation, Department of Anthropology, Brandeis University, 1998.

Bala, P. *Changing Borders and Identities in the Kelabit Highlands: Anthropological Reflections on Growing up in a Kelabit Village near the International Border.* Dayak Studies Contemporary Series, no. 1, The Institute of East Asian Studies, Universiti Malaysia Sarawak, 2002.

Chin, Lucas. *Cultural Heritage of Sarawak.* Kuching: Sarawak Museum, 1980.

Crain, Jay B. and Vicki Pearson-Rounds. "Wet Rice in Inner Borneo: The Social and Physical Ecology of the Lun Dayeh/Lun Bawang Lati' Ba System". In *Rural Development and Social Sciences Research: Case Studies from Borneo*, edited by V. T. King. BRC Proceeding Series no. 6. Phillips: Borneo Research Council, 1999, pp. 321–35.

Harrisson, T. *The World Within: A Borneo Story.* London: Cresset Press, 1959.

Hudson, Southwell C. *Uncharted Waters.* Calgary, Canada: Astana Publishing, 1999.

Janowski, M. *Rice, Work and Community Among the Kelabits in Sarawak, East Malaysia.* Ph.D. thesis. London School of Economics, University of London, 1991.

Lee, B. T. and Tengku Shamsul Bahrin. "The Bario Exodus: A Conception of Sarawak Urbanization". *Borneo Review* 4, no. 2 (December 1993): 112–27. Institute for Development Studies.

Murang, Ose. *Migration in Sarawak — The Kelabit Experience.* Presented at a Workshop On Migration in Sarawak organized by the Sarawak Development Institute, 25–26 June 1998 at Parkcity Beverly Hotel, Bintulu.

Rubenstein, Carol. "Poems of the Indigenous People of Sarawak: Some Songs and Chants (Part I and Part II)". *Sarawak Museum Journal* 21, no. 42 (1973) Special Monograph no. 2.

Rubenstein, Carol. "The Flying Silver Message Stick: Update 1985–1986 on Long Songs Collected in 1971–1974". *Sarawak Museum Journal* XLII, no. 63 (1991).

Rousseau, J. "Central Borneo and its Relations with Coastal Malay Sultanate". In

Outwitting the State, edited by P. Skalnik. New Brunswick: Transaction Publishers, 1989, pp. 41–50.

Rousseau, J. *Central Borneo: Ethnic Identity and Social Life in a Stratified Society*. Oxford: Claredon Press, 1990.

Saging, Robert Lian. "An Ethno-history of the Kelabits Tribe of Sarawak. A Brief Look at the Kelabit before World War II and after". *Borneo Research Bulletin* 2, no. 1 (1979): 14 –19.

Talla, Y. *The Kelabits of the Kelabit Highlands, Sarawak*. Provisional Research Report no. 9, Pulau Pinang: Social Anthropology Section, School of Comparative Social Sciences, University Sains Malaysia, 1979.

8

Conclusion

Hew Cheng Sim

In each chapter we have examined the multi-faceted consequences of urbanization on a specific group of women, the price paid and the rewards earned. However, three main themes have emerged from our research. The first is that gender is embedded in social transformative processes such as urbanization, but how women and men participate and experience such forces is often uneven across class, ethnicity, age, marital status and location. One thing is clear, it is more difficult for the poor, lowly educated rural migrant women who are mainly the subjects of this book, to negotiate this terrain of change than their better educated middle-class, urban sisters. The second theme is that although new opportunities for women arise, pre-existing gender inequality such as poverty, economic exploitation and discrimination is often exacerbated by rapid social change. The third theme is that elderly village mothers and city daughters who face insurmountable obstacles often must turn to their poverty-stricken families for support. The inadequacy of state intervention to ensure the survival of these fragile families is pivotal to women's experiences of the disempowering aspects of macro-structural changes.

Single women enjoy greater mobility and therefore expanded employment opportunities in the cities than their married sisters who remain in the village. However, in a gender-segmented labour market, women with low education and limited marketable skills find themselves at a disadvantaged position in comparison to their brothers in the same strata. Women earn less, have lower occupational mobility and experience more discrimination. In addition, they suffer greater sexual vulnerability in the urban courtship game. When they marry and have children, new dependencies are created when they have to withdraw from the labour market and become family caretakers. If their marriage or relationship fails, unemployment and low wages translate into poverty for single mothers. It is pertinent to add here that the vulnerability of women in marriages or liaisons in recent times is also a consequence of urbanization and men's greater labour mobility. Women's important contribution to the well-being and future of society should be acknowledged and official policies and plans should identify and promote benefits to women. Sustained and committed public policies are required to ameliorate women's situation.

In contrast to their poor, uneducated sisters, women migrants to cities with higher levels of education find that it both alienates them from their village background and liberates them to urban opportunities. Educational achievement is the key reason for migration amongst Kelabit and is viewed as an avenue for upward mobility. As the Kelabit has a long history of migration to towns and cities, the stress of adaptation to urban lifestyles is reduced because earlier migrants act as support networks for later migrants. However, it is a different experience for village mothers left behind. They suffer increased workloads, emotional loss when their daughters leave and when elderly, become vulnerable to neglect. In a significant departure from the norm, rural elderly women have a shorter life expectancy than men. In order to escape such a fate, some elderly village mothers migrate to join their children in the cities. While some are able to adjust to city living and enjoy a higher standard of healthcare there, others are alienated by the urban environment. In the most disempowering circumstances, women's subordinate position and the stresses of rapid social transformation have led to an increase in the diagnosis of women's mental illness. The gendered treatment of this group of women both by the community and by psychiatric institutions points to fear and intolerance of women's sexuality.

Hence the path of women in their encounters with urbanization is ambivalent, contradictory and fraught with difficulties. It is left to other researchers in the future to study how women push the boundaries to win greater opportunities and to negotiate choices for themselves in the face of such rapid social transformation. No matter which group of women we have encountered in this book, one fact remains: each has to walk the tightrope between rural and urban and each has to struggle with loss and gain so as to come to terms with what it means to survive in a turbulent world.

Index

www.ingramcontent.com/pod-product-compliance
Lightning Source LLC
Chambersburg PA
CBHW021539260326
41914CB00001B/84